T0311395

"In the trilogy that concludes with *The Authority of Tenderness*, Paul Williams proves himself a fearless explorer of some of the darkest reaches of the human psyche."

– JM Coetzee

"This third book of Paul Williams' trilogy—a book at once fiction, nonfiction and memoir—is like no other work I have ever read. Williams' use of language unobtrusively achieves the music of poetry and the enlightened absurdity of Beckett. Even in the most dark, most disturbing parts of this book, there lives a thread of hope that is safeguarded by the potential of the human spirit for 'the authority of tenderness'. This book offers an experience in reading not to be missed."

– Thomas Ogden

"This final volume in the trilogy by Paul Williams is a searing journey into the heart of darkness. As a psychoanalyst who has treated disturbed patients throughout his career, Williams shares his unique and brilliant way of being with these individuals that helps them to live with themselves and with others. His creative use of the concept of tenderness is novel and original in this context. I highly recommend this gem of a book for all psychoanalysts and psychotherapists of patients who struggle to emerge from the darkness."

– Glen O. Gabbard, MD

"Each sentence of this book is constructed with exceptional depth and acuity. Traumatized individuals bear the unbearable, the authentic self exposed to unthinkable anxiety. Paul Williams reflects on his experience and that as a psychoanalyst of severely traumatized patients. His path to the patient's authentic self through the authority exercised by the clinician's tenderness is profoundly moving, of great clinical value not only to psychoanalysts but to all individuals who wonder about the problematic nature of human existence."

– Franco De Masi

"Donald Winnicott wrote of a state of inward being that requires the utmost privacy. Intrusions into this most intimate of places can result in a violent destruction of personality. The result can be a total catastrophe. This is surely among the most important themes in psychoanalysis. Paul Williams, writing out of personal experience as well as out of a long-time experience as a psychoanalyst, considers what Yeats called 'the deep heart's core' with a sonority and depth of feeling that puts me in mind of masterly music making."

– Eric Rhode, author and retired psychotherapist

THE AUTHORITY OF
TENDERNESS

This insightful and beautifully written work explores nonlinear processes of recovery of the loss of Self. The inherent healing power of hard-earned, wholehearted self-acceptance is conceived through the authority of tenderness.

The book is the final volume in *The Fifth Principle* trilogy (the second book being *Scum*), which chronicled, through the course of one boy's lifetime, the methods of a mind which is not a mind, in its efforts to prevail under oppressive circumstances. *The Authority of Tenderness* comes at the end of the journey, is written by the adult self of the child, and uses poetic vignettes, references to foundational psychoanalytic literature and analyses of critical treatment situations to convey the experiences of someone who has been both patient and analyst.

The book offers a vivid psychotherapeutic perspective for clinicians, trainees, students and general readers alike.

Paul Williams trained as a psychoanalyst with The British Psychoanalytical Society where he was a training analyst and, from 2001 to 2007, joint editor-in-chief of the *International Journal of Psychoanalysis*. He was a consultant psychotherapist in the National Health Service in Belfast, Northern Ireland. Since 2016 he has lived and worked in private psychoanalytic practice in Northern California. He has published widely on the subject of severe disturbance. *The Authority of Tenderness* follows *The Fifth Principle* (Routledge, 2010) and *Scum* (Routledge, 2013).

THE AUTHORITY
OF TENDERNESS
Dignity and the True Self in Psychoanalysis

Paul Williams

Routledge
Taylor & Francis Group

LONDON AND NEW YORK

First published 2022
by Routledge
2 Park Square, Milton Park, Abingdon, Oxon OX14 4RN

and by Routledge
605 Third Avenue, New York, NY 10158

Routledge is an imprint of the Taylor & Francis Group, an informa business

British Library Cataloguing-in-Publication Data
A catalogue record for this book is available from the British Library

Library of Congress Cataloging-in-Publication Data
Names: Williams, Paul (Psychotherapist), author.
Title: The authority of tenderness : dignity and the true self in
psychoanalysis / Paul Williams.
Description: Abingdon, Oxon ; New York, NY : Routledge, 2022. | Includes
bibliographical references and index. | Summary: "This insightful and beautifully
written work explores non-linear processes of recovery of the loss of Self. The
inherent healing power of hard-earned, wholehearted self-acceptance is conceived
through the authority of tenderness. The book offers a vivid psychotherapeutic
perspective for clinicians, trainees, students and general readers alike"—Provided
by publisher.
Identifiers: LCCN 2021023126 (print) | LCCN 2021023127 (ebook) |
ISBN 9781032009759 (hardback) | ISBN 9781032009360 (paperback) |
ISBN 9781003176862 (ebook)
Subjects: LCSH: Self. | Self-acceptance. | Psychoanalysis. | Psychotherapy.
Classification: LCC BF697 .W4947 2022 (print) | LCC BF697 (ebook) |
DDC 150.19/5—dc23
LC record available at https://lccn.loc.gov/2021023126
LC ebook record available at https://lccn.loc.gov/2021023127

ISBN: 978-1-032-00975-9 (hbk)
ISBN: 978-1-032-00936-0 (pbk)
ISBN: 978-1-003-17686-2 (ebk)

DOI: 10.4324/9781003176862

Typeset in Times New Roman and Helvetica Neue Ultra Light
by Apex CoVantage, LLC

For O and L

CONTENTS

This book is the last of a trilogy that began with *The Fifth Principle* and was followed by *Scum*. The first two books examined the experiences of a child. Neither book could have been written by the child and required a spokesperson. This book is written by and on behalf of the adult self of that child. The measure of its worth will, as before, be the extent to which it enters the lived experience of the reader.

I am grateful to Thomas Ogden and Eric Rhode for their help. Without the encouragement of J.M. Coetzee, this trilogy might not have seen the light of day.

PREFACE

In the early 2000s, after a considerable number of years treating seriously disturbed individuals psychoanalytically, successfully and unsuccessfully, I became increasingly aware, as have some before me, of the limitations of existing psychoanalytic concepts and techniques when working with such patients. I also became aware of certain significant limitations in myself. Fairbairn, Winnicott, Bion, Beckett, Tolstoy, Dostoevsky and an analysis led me, amongst other things, to write, in 2009, the first volume of a trilogy of pieces of literature (of which this book is the final part) concerning the loss of self and processes of reclamation. The first book (*The Fifth Principle*) took as its subject experiences originating in my own life between birth and 8 or 9 years of age. This was not autobiography or a 'case history', because the author of the book and the individual about which the book is written are not the same person. The book is a piece of literature furnishing an account of the methods of one particular mind in its efforts to prevail under oppressive circumstances. The author undertook, on behalf of the subject, to provide a faithful, intelligible rendering of unintelligible events. The mind in question, insofar as it resembles other minds, was given an opportunity to speak to the reader, which could not have happened in reality, in ways that might be recognizable, though some of the things that were written about might be unfamiliar. The extent to which the account finds a home in the mind and imagination of the reader is the measure of its worth. Another way of putting it is that the purpose of the book was to try to convey *experiences* of childhood that could not otherwise be talked about.

The second book (*Scum*) continued a similar theme in order to capture the experiences of a panic-stricken adolescent, the later self of the individual in the first book, as he attempted to negotiate the demands of an utterly senseless world. Disjuncture, cruelty and terror are characterized by fragmented language in the book within which echo primitive experiences, capturing not only the psychosis that is everyday adolescence but also what happens when isolation and brutality add to this chaos. By great good fortune, this boy was spirited to rural France at the age of 17 where his own humanity became apparent and elements of a foundation for a life materialized.

This third and final book in the trilogy differs from the previous two books in that it is written by the adult self of the young individuals written about earlier and takes into account five further decades of experience. Its content varies between types of experiences needed by a disturbed individual to recover and the actual experience of the recovery. Although concepts, theories and ideas are important in psychoanalysis and play a part in all clinical work, this book is neither theoretical nor does it seek to teach anything. It is a glimpse into processes of change – actual, lived experiences which, if respected, address one of the most fundamental concerns facing psychoanalysis today, and certainly the greatest preoccupation of tormented and confused individuals. This is the question of the dignity of the true self. We all possess a unique and inexplicable true self which, as commentators from Meister Eckhart to Winnicott have emphasized, is a hallowed ground requiring seclusion and lack of interference if mental and psychological health is to be founded and maintained. Paradoxically, it is only through deference to this psychological condition that the individual's personality is permitted to connect, develop and prosper with others. Even a precis of complex developmental needs like this one reveals numerous implications for psychoanalytic therapy. Practicing psychoanalysis could be likened to restoring a painting. Patient and analyst attempt together to lift the grime and wear of the years without damaging the original. Where damage appears, repair is carefully undertaken in accordance with, as far as possible, the intentions of the creator – the Self of the patient. The process may have qualities of a science, but it is definitely an art. Successful analysis, in my opinion, draws a distinction between the developmental Self of the individual, in need of assistance, and the True Self, in need of solitude and dignity. Failure to make this distinction was conveyed by a late friend in a way that I have never heard put better. He had a training analysis when he was much younger with an eminent analyst who, after 5 years' work with him, died. In grief and in need of help, it was suggested he see another, not quite so eminent, analyst but someone revered for her clinical skill. He told me: 'My second analyst was a better analyst in some respects, but she pulled out my psychopathology by the roots. My first analyst knew me, too, but she was more kind'. He felt damaged by the second, more 'accurate' analysis. Perhaps science had taken precedence over art. His first analyst had

had a sensibility to his core vulnerabilities and strengths – his true self – and had respected these. His second analyst had failed to respect the dignity of his true self.

For seriously disturbed individuals, the dilemma of how to live reflects the scale and nature of internal damage. The origins of disturbance are many and varied, but the individual's response to it is what brings the person into analytic therapy, to save his or her life and with some hope for meaningful change. My respect for individuals who undertake such work remains undimmed. The gravest consequence of having suffered serious disturbance is exposure of the true self. The dissolution of personality is imminent when this arises and it presents the clinician with the greatest of responsibilities. Assessing the degree of integrity of the personality, including the true self, is necessary to grasp what can or cannot be expected of the individual. To overlook this form of assessment incurs the risk of riding roughshod over the vulnerabilities of the true self, worsening the patient's condition and, at best, inducing adaptation to the defensive needs of a damaged self. In this book, in different ways, I speak to the need to attend to the privacy and dignity of the true self. If this is accomplished, both parties are freed to pursue as much analysis as the personality needs, especially the need to experience outrage in response to impingements on the true self.

Paul Williams
Greenbrae, California
October 2020

1

SOLITUDE

Solitude, founded on silence to settle the soul, reveals its intelligence as we listen, without thought. The silence of solitude is not an absence of sound but the pulse of life, confiding off the record, without explanation or knowledge, from infinite orbit and depth, what matters. This is wonder, the activity at our core. Unhurried, we listen through the silence to that which, unknowable, molds symbols from wonder, for no reason or purpose, whatever we do, work, sleep, play, cook, sing, put out garbage.

Solitude is not loneliness, estrangement, alienation, withdrawal, resignation or isolation. It is privacy, with everyone present. No one who matters is left out. No one who doesn't matter is left out. A proviso for wonder, solitude seems to lie behind all that is creative, itself the descendant of wonder in the realm of the unthinkable. Each of us is new and unique, unlike any before or after. To be creative in solitude is the experience of a close encounter with wonder through our unique, authentic self. What makes each creative moment original and unrepeatable is its intrinsically personal origin and unthought, transcendent span. Timeless, it leaves its mark on our life and the lives of others.

DOI: 10.4324/9781003176862-1   1

Wonder, like all authentic experiences, occurs when we are nothing other than who we are. When we classify, analyze, talk or write about experiences, we are uprooted. The truth of what you are reading now is worthless unless you admit, without reason, the experience of wonder in your Self, the intent of which is to withhold no experience or person, to remain whole.[1] We cannot fully know ourselves, or any other person, because genuine, core selves need to remain unknown, prior to knowledge, and be lived as experiences about which we wonder.

As we develop, patterns are laid down contiguous to the authentic self which has no concern for communication, let alone engagement. Experience of others involves departure from our authentic self which could be depleting, so a way of growing is needed which, under favorable circumstances, comes naturally, if not always easily. A true relationship must entail acceptance of the authentic self in ourselves and in others in order to deepen. This is not always possible. The parent (or person) who says to a child (or person) *'I love you but not how you are behaving'* conflates self with behavior whilst believing they are not doing this and, in so doing, rejects the entire child/person. We are not made up of elements that can be suppressed or enhanced, rejected or accepted. We are inherently, originally whole and strive to protect this wholeness and integrity whatever else happens to us. Exposing and assaulting the authentic self is a mutilation, including for the perpetrator. Even in those who plan suicide, the idea of continuing to exist following suicide is a sane, albeit desperate, attempt to not forsake wholeness. We possess an indwelling, abiding sense of our own self and, from this, the self in others, even if we are unable to make use of it. No matter how disaffected or estranged we feel, this integrity is inviolate.

When accepted and respected, our authentic self sanctions constructive engagement with others, including in adversity and conflict. Appreciation of the authentic self without thought or reason may be the most natural form of love there is and an essential underpinning for the courage required to face conflict. Resolution of conflict requires negotiation of extreme feelings, competing urges and irrational as well as rational wishes and cannot succeed without regard for the authentic self in oneself and the other. The sober tenderness of this intelligence is the strategic authority for repair.

Wonder, an experience that is unpredictable and disquieting, enlivens like no other. We wonder 'about something' only for it to disperse, scatter to the four winds, leaving in its wake wonder about what we have been wondering about. Is wonder the primary, private force through which we shape ourselves? When accorded the solitude and spontaneity it thrives upon, wonder treats us as longed-for beneficiaries and, when passed over, it waits patiently as it sees more clearly than we do that we are the something and the something else being wondered about, without thinking or knowing. It is an embrace without which we are unable to live life.

Solitude and wonder are drawn to each other like friends comparing notes, musing, improvising, doing nothing. And we? We let them get on with it. The partnership arose prior to us, in the eyes of a mother filled with a vision of the wholeness of her newborn baby, an aliveness maintained by respectful wonder that engenders the person who is her child.

The isolated person does not have this partnership, or the experience of respect for the authentic self. Confusion as to what constitutes a relationship is inevitable. Esteem by others for the authentic self may be misconstrued as distance or neglect, connection as intrusion and invasion, safety as withdrawal, kinship as psychosis. Notwithstanding this suffering, the isolated individual continues to be lived by an elemental sentience of the authentic self, which is the birthplace of hope. Hope relies upon isolation of the core, authentic self which releases the personality in search of the lifeblood of dependence on the other. Isolation of the authentic self, essential for health, lies in marked contrast to *radical* isolation in which 'psychic pseudopodia' from the infant seeking out nutrients from the environment were met by nothing or toxins, provoking retreat by the core self into ever deeper hiding. Solitude, partnership and wonder are beyond reach. If the core self is forced to give itself up, the mind collapses, along with the personality. Those who survive such compromises of the will to live are at constant risk of splintering, there being 'no one inside' to assist the personality. They live in fear and despair, a despair that can feel like a contagion.

A temptation for the personality with a healthily isolated authentic self is to ignore the unavailability of the radically isolated individual who has 'no one inside'. There is nothing much there, is there? Or what is there is 'bad'. The truth is, what is there is not what there is. What there is, unavailable to both parties, is an authentic self not insulated but exposed and violated.

The authority of tenderness, devoid of thinking and reason, is needed by the body and mind of the isolated individual so that respect for the authentic self may be established. Neither party will necessarily enjoy what may be painful labor, but nothing the radically isolated person does is capable of withstanding the authority of tenderness, because there is nothing to withstand. Its lifeblood is the safety the authentic self depends upon, even if the personality imagines it can't bear it. The authority of tenderness possesses no power or influence beyond fair-minded recognition. At its most difficult, the individual's response might be anguish that surprises or strickens the starved personality. This is not fundamental opposition but more a shock to the system, like the person dying of thirst who coughs and vomits from taking in too much water. At its best, there may be wordless affiliation.

Why do all this? is the question in the minds of both parties. Because it makes it possible to create, by respecting the authentic self, an experience of shared wonder, a combination of solitude and intimate partnership which is the unique vision of where we began.

Loneliness is a good thing. When we are radically isolated, we cannot experience loneliness or the need for another. Loneliness is an unattainable luxury. When the authentic self is imperiled and lacks protection, others are what we believe we need least. The personality's 'pseudo-podia' are withdrawn from contact, including from internal others. Until the authority of tenderness prevails and the true self is granted the acceptance and solitude it needs, the mind and personality are caged and subjugated. It takes time for the authority of tenderness to inscribe itself. The individual may have been incapacitated by radical isolation and the authentic self may appear to have disintegrated, but respect for its dignity and thoughtful interest in the suffering of the individual are the conditions for a resumption of living, not existing, and from these experiences, loneliness may become achievable.

Note

1 When asked to explain short-story writing, Flannery O'Connor replied: 'Asking me to talk about story-writing is just like asking a fish to lecture on swimming' (O'Connor, 1969, p. 87).

2

ISOLATION REVISITED

In physiological development cells are capable of becoming any number of things, then some things, then one thing. Division occurs using an isolating principle that is necessary for differentiation – a general function splits progressively into a diversity of specialized functions. In psychological development there is an analogous situation beginning with a form of unity that gives way to progressive differentiation. There is, however, an important difference. The core self (the authentic or true self, reflecting the individual's unique integrity) that begins life *in utero* remains preserved and undiscovered as differentiation proceeds and the individual strives to fulfil his or her potential. During this development this core state is not given up to differentiation but is the condition for it.

Donald Winnicott used the term *isolate* to describe the unique, authentic self that needs to be protected and not be found but at the same time allows relating to others to proceed if healthy growth is to take place. He suggested that the isolate's origins lie in the infant's helpless dependence from the outset. The creation of the breast (life) in imagination endows the infant with a sense of inventive

DOI: 10.4324/9781003176862-2

power that is the source of artistic inspiration and creativity in ordinary life. This hidden, newborn 'creator' must not be found or exposed in life or in psychoanalysis:

> *At the centre of each person is an incommunicado element, and this is most sacred and worthy of preservation. . . . I would say that the traumatic experiences that lead to the organization of primitive defences belong to the threat to the isolated core, the threat of its being found, altered, communicated with. The defence consists in a further hiding of the secret self, even in the extreme to its projection and to its endless dissemination. . . . Rape, and being eaten by cannibals, these are mere bagatelles as compared with the violation of the self's core, the alteration of the self's central elements by communication seeping through the defenses. For me this would be the sin against the self. (Winnicott, 1963, p. 187)*

The paradox to which he points implies challenges for growth of the person that affect both the safety of the authentic self and the health of the developing mind. These are daunting for everyone, and nowhere more so than for those whose isolate has been 'discovered' or assaulted. The impact of interference with the authentic self gives rise to dread of human contact, leading to radical isolation. Aloneness is needed by the authentic self for it to remain healthy. There is no greater state of helpless dependence than the experience of prenatal life and the ensuing postnatal days, weeks and months of infancy. Interaction between infant and mother prior to birth in which the mother attunes to her baby, and at the same time the fetus 'gets to know' the mother from the inside, is a natural matrix for incubation of the authentic self and future personality. It is not unreasonable to think of this form of relating as giving rise to the earliest incarnations of temperament and interpersonal life.

To develop a capacity to relate to another person is a cumulative (lifelong) internal and interpersonal experience. Adaptation cannot facilitate this development or promote growth of an independent personality. The demand for external affirmation to regulate poor self-esteem cannot substitute for trustworthy internal and external relationships. Basic trust in the acceptance of one's inherent *wholeness*, the unique integrity that defines the authentic self, is the foundation from which a capacity to relate develops. Assisting a severely troubled person to change while avoiding violation of that person's authentic self is a highly complex undertaking, because basic trust is missing. One pitfall that is commonly overlooked is an assumption that isolation, or an individual's need for privacy, is a symptom of underlying illness. We may consider interpretation to be an antidote to this and, to do this, ask to hear 'everything'. The person may feel obliged to accept these ideas as to what constitutes healthy talk and relating and so yield private information not voluntarily but according to an imperative that to not do so is failure. Many thoughts pass through my mind that are elusive, poorly formed, or *in potentia*. They can be frightening, shaming, confusing or plain incoherent. That I must reveal *all* of them, come what may, seems to me a blunt instrument that could further expose and compromise my authentic self, leading to more, not less, isolation, especially if my authentic self has already been compromised. We are all entitled to keep certain things private.

Isolation prevents change if the authentic self has been subjected to exposure, but when this self is treated with respect, it may produce change and emergence of an alive personality. Inordinate reverence for the authentic self is not required. Extreme unease about being direct may fore-close forms of contact that are helpful for change. Communication via the authority of tenderness is directed at the personality of the individual *whilst taking into account* the authentic self. There is an inherent tension between the needs of the authentic self and the needs of the evolving personality which, if attended to, builds a foundation for becoming a human being.

A boy

An abused, isolated boy attends, for the first time in his feral life, a celebratory social gathering (Williams, 2010). There is a pianist and singing takes place, including of the Beatles song 'Yellow Submarine'. The boy, on hearing the happy music, becomes distraught and panics, finds a corner, and sobs uncontrollably. He is lost, moved and overtaken by wild grief, with no mind to assimilate what is taking place. A concerned couple usher the boy into a side room and the woman asks,

'What is wrong?'

The boy, now probably in a state of psychotic confusion, struggles mutely to respond to the woman's gentle but seri-ous question, before finally blurting out, *'The farmer shot my dog'*. He has no idea why he says this, because he has no dog, yet the statement turns out to be of importance, con-veying the truth of his plight that was known yet unknown to him. He had been senselessly murdered. He communicated this murder in a form akin to a haiku poem. The woman reacts with sympathy. *'That's terrible'*, she says.

On hearing this, the boy's panic escalates to unbearable intensity. With no words or thoughts, only an ear-splitting accusation of being a filthy liar for coming up with such a story, and on the brink of mortifying shame, he flees, bolting through the gathering of people and running far away, as far as he can get from the building; from her; and, above all, from himself. The communication and noncommunication between these two alien species illustrate a profound failure in the boy of establishment of and respect for the isolation needed to protect his core self, the basis of his mental health. The privations caused by massive, early, internal upheaval placed this defenceless boy at continuous risk of being exposed and of descent into insanity.

He could not run far or fast enough to escape the imminent catastrophe of feeling connected, yet the fact that he had let slip a profound truth in response to the sensitive woman's question remained unequivocal. *'The farmer shot my dog'* was not a haiku or metaphor or memory but a form of unwilled openness from his deepest being – the core self. It collided, without the protection of psychological defences, with a different universe evoked by a tender maternal figure absorbed in her child's distress. It was a connection the boy needed desperately but could neither recognize nor understand nor bear.

His universe, devoid of benign figures, was a *bricolage* of raw emotion, unrequited longings, fragments of primitive thought and instinctive survival mechanisms. He lived in torment, hated life, dreaded death and coped by numbing himself to anything beyond moment-to-moment survival. Yet something in him, in this authentically human context, had revealed the appalling truth of his situation. The shattering congeniality of the gathering and the woman's sincere concern for him split wide open a pre-existing fissure that spewed out a raw response, exposing the isolate. His use of imagery might have been put differently had he been a person, say, through metaphor, association or a dream image that could be thought about, but he did not live in a world of reality or of persons. This is why his concrete response is not explainable as paranoid or the product of psychotic thinking, which it may well have also been.

The boy knew at best only nominally of a world of connection and nothing about the need for dependence as an infant, which allows for protection of the authentic self and differentiation of the personality. His authentic self had not been protected, and his needs had been disregarded. He lived in the world so realistically that growth of an inner world had been vitiated and his authentic self remained at continuous risk of exposure and injury. Is this why he reacted to the woman with shock and horror and not fear of his or her 'murderousness'? The woman's engagement with him, alien though it was, seared him with its kindness, exposing his authentic self *to him* and mortifying him. The boy did not react with horror to the woman herself: she was a total stranger, and persons were a homogenous category anyway, to be kept at bay. He reacted physically and with dismay to the visceral sound and unconscious import of her embodied, related words that conveyed a capacity for deep human connection he agonized over yet knew nothing about. He fled when her much needed, developmental 'life blood' scalded his icy, private wilderness. Fear of his own extinction, not because the woman was his enemy but because her care was experienced as physical agony in his organs, demanded that he put as much distance as possible between his authentic self, this excruciating threat and himself. In her tenderness, she knew not to pursue him or shout after him. He had not known he would be risking death by speaking to her. A human being was the only thing that could save him, but it was also what had killed him, and here it was happening again.

The boy's authentic self had been found, altered and disfigured in infancy, before he was able to protect himself. His yearning to experience what a mother was really like momentarily overrode his terror. Perhaps he was feeling suicidal and there was nothing to lose. Whatever his motivation, his pursuit of truth and his outrage toward the murderer ('the farmer') gave him an intimation of how human contact might be possible but at the unforeseen risk of a repetition of the killing. The struggle to tell the untellable truth, which he never lost, may have protected him from becoming chronically mentally ill.

Many have to fight to preserve the integrity and privacy of the authentic self. The destructive isolation of this particular boy had been compounded by assaults, bullying and self-hatred, and these had disbarred him from humanization. Retreat by the core self into ever deeper hiding had allowed his incipient mind to become corrupted. He made pacts with aggressors, internal and external, in confused, last-ditch attempts to preserve his authentic self. Fortunately for him, the woman who intervened was an apparition of all he had missed and hungered for, which may have been worth the agony. If the core self is forced to give itself up to a hostile, invasive individual, the person collapses and the self dies, or commits suicide, in reality or psychically, leaving a barely functioning body or a corpse. When the will to live is compromised in this way, what is left survives at continuous risk of harm by others or oneself.

Practices of torture rely upon exposure of the core self. Psychological death occurs via merger with the torturer, the subject 'becoming' the torturer, murdering themselves and then others (Williams, 2010, 2014). The phenomenon of the concentration camp 'Musulmann' is a graphic example of exposure of the core self. Levi (1961) described Musulmen as

> . . . *an anonymous mass, continuously renewed and always identical, of no-men who marched and labored in silence, the divine spark dead within them, already too empty really to suffer . . . the weak, the infirm, those who were doomed to be singled out for the gas chambers. (p. 103)*

What kinds of mental states existed in individuals who were tortured into becoming Musulmen, compared to those who were not? Could torturers, including contemporary soul-murderers, make use of the primordial knowledge I have tried to describe to identify their victims? Torturers and bullies may know instinctively how to recognize signs of exposure of the authentic self that communicates helplessness. The paucity of study of predatory invasion of minds may be one reason why these still widespread practices are underreported.

Narcissism is viewed as the sickness that defines the age. If this is so, it is not difficult to see how this would carry implications for the authentic self. Narcissism is a demand to become someone else and is a close relative of insanity. Survival, for the narcissist, depends upon submission, leaving little room for adequate protection of the authentic self. An authentic self that is threatened by narcissistic assault from inside or outside lies in perpetual danger of violation.

If this is not identified by the mental health worker, the integrity of the person and what might be expected of them cannot be assessed. Riding roughshod over the vulnerability of the authentic self is not uncommon, including by those who have been highly trained to deal with mental illness.

Assault of the authentic self is discernible in insanity by withdrawal from relationships into reliance upon an internal fantasy life and gratifying feelings that derive from, and which fuel, thinking that is out of touch with the pains of human reality. This withdrawal damages the mind and personality extensively, leaving the authentic self unprotected and in search of ever deeper retreat. A seductive world of hallucinated sensations is employed to protect against assault and pain whilst fostering the very conditions for it.

How do we talk with an individual living in an alien reality established in infancy when the 'pseudopodia' of the budding authentic self sought out nutrients from the environment only to find nothing or else poison, thereby creating the conditions for *radical* isolation? Listening, not talking or instructing, is primary. 'Echolocation', for example, is a form of listening *through* the sound and meaning of what the individual says to what they cannot say directly, not due to defensive psychological activity, which can take place, or because meaning is unconscious, which it also is, but because the core quandary the person is experiencing existed prior to, and deep within, the earliest stages of articulation of connections between the subject, the authentic self and another person. The plight being communicated concerns an authentic self in crisis that is neither capable of nor helped by communication, because its role is to not be seen, found or communicated with. The personality, meanwhile, lies in urgent need of help. Echolocation, a 'sonar'

15

activity,[1] is an indirect form of listening receptive to traces of the authentic self that may have been compromised by the severe distress of exposure and left in dread of being exposed further. These traces may be discernible through primordial cries and whispers; idiosyncratic fears filtered through eccentric or deranged ideas; oblique, 'poetic' statements; odd allusions or prolonged silences. A characteristic of this type of (non)communicating is its quality of timelessness. 'Eternal refrains' hint at pressing, unreachable enigmas using words tangentially and reluctantly, words felt to be bankrupt in the face of such impasse. A 'gestalt' around a core, ceaseless preoccupation with something unreachable has left the sufferer endlessly laid bare.

In less deeply troubled individuals we might think of these vulnerabilities as 'personality traits' based on complex or painful life events that seep out over time and are to be viewed as aspects of 'character' or 'temperament', not necessarily in need of urgent investigation. We place faith in the integrative potential of mental functions and a capacity for dependency, differentiation and individuation as pathways to reduce the impact of these vulnerabilities. Yet severely damaged individuals do not have the good fortune of these forms of mental protection. The authentic self, having been exposed, places the subject in fear of extinction, a difficult experience to imagine.

Communicating authentically with such a person requires exposure of *oneself* to comparable forms of unexpected grief, hopelessness, confusion and dismay, and sometimes to bodily symptoms like nausea, fatigue, tearfulness, hostile agitation or visceral abhorrence (as though organs could howl). We are pulled into these states to the point of feeling overwhelmed, humbled and powerless, whilst feeling greatly concerned, although about what is not always clear.

No matter how we formulate ideas from these unusual experiences to help the person become more human, we will be sharing these ideas with *someone other than the person with whom we are speaking*. In this unusual process we can remain alert for intimations of truth, reconciled to doubt and attentive to messages that are inexplicable or seem forged from an unknown language. We use the medium of our own uncertain, available personality as a channel to impart, with honesty, a sounding to the domain of the authentic self, without explanation, challenge or need for dialogue. What may become discussable is the other medium's uncertain translation of any such communication, insofar as the two parties are able to decipher this. If the listener is able to sustain this depth of responsiveness whilst maintaining restraint, it may be possible for the authentic self to have an experience of its sacrosanct isolation being treated with respect. Psychic pseudopodia, withdrawn but not atrophied, are then provided with the conditions to seek out life-giving nutrients. These pseudopodia, sanctioned to proceed in the direction of the other, create conditions for the healthy isolation of the authentic self through the personality's experience of dependence on another person. The task I describe is, of course, difficult and demands levels of patience that exceed those required with a person who has not undergone such deprivation and assault.

A woman

A woman I got to know told me about how as a child she'd taken care of her mentally ill mother. She was one of six children and numerous miscarriages. Her mother was frequently hospitalized when she became physically and verbally violent in the belief that her husband, children or neighbours wanted to kill her. The father escaped into alcohol. The woman/child soothed her mother and tended to her many ailments. All of her siblings have become mentally ill and one committed suicide. She talked to me in friendly, if disjointed, ways about all of this. As we got to know each other she became less friendly and somewhat forlorn, lapsing into silences and more disorientated language. She had a way of confusing me by agreeing and disagreeing at the same time with things I said. This happened regularly and always took me by surprise. She also agreed with things I had *not* said. For example, she might disagree with something I had said but which I couldn't recall, so I imagined I had forgotten it. She might then agree with something I definitely knew I *hadn't* said, and I felt in complete confusion as to what was real. I surmised initially that she was trying to make me not see something she genuinely didn't agree with, but as I got to know her, mainly through my own incoherent experiences, I came to see that behind her bizarre speech was a person who did not know anything about having a genuine conversation with another person. She let me know that she'd always had great difficulty talking with people. I began to wonder whether she had given up on people, given the unreality of her behaviour. She did not seem to feel angry or hurt about her plight but rather felt unentitled to talk or have anything for herself, including a life. Any strong feeling seemed out of reach. She sought nothing, except perhaps survival, and it occurred to me that she was waiting for her existence to run its unhappy course. When any trace of feeling arose in her she seemed to believe it led nowhere and released herself from its tender pull. Her forlorn lifelessness did not allow for animation or rebellion against her plight. She could be cold and distant but never resentful.

One evening, to my great surprise, she called me in a terrible state. I learned later that a female friend with whom she had been cycling in a group had suffered an extremely serious accident whilst moving to the centre of the road to indicate that the group was about to make a turn. She was struck from behind by a car overtaking at speed and her injuries were extensive and life-threatening. When she called me, all I could hear was a primitive wailing. No words, just howling. I asked her to tell me, if she could, what had happened, but she couldn't speak. Using broken syllables, she conveyed something about an accident. I ascertained that she herself wasn't harmed, asked that she make sure she wasn't alone and suggested we talk the following morning. We met as arranged and the wailing resumed – an ululating, animal-like pain. My attempts to reach her made things worse. She seemed as exposed as the friend who had been almost killed. I felt my sole option was to remain silent whilst attentive to her distress. Eerily, and without warning, she became calm and began describing the accident calmly and without feeling, as though reading about it from a newspaper. I felt shaken and disoriented. After much reflection, I realized that her wailing could not be explained purely as communication of distress about her friend. It was a ruptured agony that had to be sutured at all costs, because it had exposed her authentic self to a degree that was beyond human endurance. When I voiced my concern for her in the light of this terrible experience she did not object but was mystified and seemed no longer interested in what had happened to her or her friend, except for emotionless platitudes. My attempts at 'echolocation' drifted into the ether. Her withdrawal into lifelessness resumed and did not change from that day on. What did happen was that she 're-grouped' during the ensuing weeks and months, becoming more committed to her work as a private tutor and taking on 'deserving' cases. She became irrationally preoccupied by her husband's (good) health, fearing he might suddenly die. She mentioned in passing to me night-mares in which she herself was worried about dying, but these were more of an irritant than a source of distress.

I concluded that the dreadful accident of her friend had dislodged and exposed her radically isolated, authentic self, revealing an intolerable horror of being annihilated. I regret that I was unable to help her with this. Despite having some acquaintances, she remained profoundly isolated. Her attention to her students and husband brought satisfaction for those involved, but it also sealed her off further from people. A good many aspects of her life seemed to proceed reasonably, but her lifeless biding of time until her existence ran its course to death continued and had, I suspect, deepened. An injunction to seal off the authentic self at the cost of an alive personality flies in the face of relating to people and to living. The outcome is disconnection from oneself and the world. For the woman I knew, respect for the integrity of her authentic self was not enough.

Note

1 *Echolocation* is a term denoting a process used for locating distant or invisible objects that employs sound waves that are sent out or reflected back to the sender by the objects themselves. Echolocation is used by animals and has been studied in humans for navigation and orientation purposes, to identify and evade obstacles, to seek out food and to assess forms of social contact. The sonar activity of echolocation is predicated upon uncertainty and unpredictability.

3

TERROR

A retired psychotherapist in the Republic of Georgia told me of a view there that the root of human psychological difficulty is fear. Of being born, irreversible differentiation, division, the unknown, loss of the good, sexuality, conflict, death. As I wondered about this, I wondered increasingly about what I was wondering about. I found myself returning to something I was unable to grasp that led me onto stony ground. This was an experience of *pervasive* fear. A sensation that there is nothing *but* fear. No matter which way I looked at it, the idea kept recurring and made no sense, even though I knew I knew about it.

One particular person's intuition revealed to me that my idea of pervasive fear might be a misnomer. A gifted professional woman in her 50s, she had suffered a psychotic illness for most of her life. Her mother had suffered a psychosis throughout her childhood. Both parents had threatened to abandon the children (there were three) and the father did, in fact, leave the family when my patient was 7, but not before co-opting her into 'caring for' her mother.

My patient's need to depend on me for help met with violent opposition in her, generating daily manipulations of

DOI: 10.4324/9781003176862-3

me and a credible resolve to kill herself which nearly succeeded. Only when I was finally obliged to give up hope of
being able to help her and to resign myself to the real possibility that she could kill herself did she begin to tell me, bit
by bit, of her terror. Over five painful years she chronicled
the 'hum of terror' with which she had lived for as long as
she could recall.

My patient was afraid she could kill me with her hatred,
but this was not the terror she was disclosing to me. Her
mother's illness had manifested itself as overdoses of
alcohol and analgesics, collapses following fits of despair,
physical illnesses, emergency hospital admissions and sud-
den departures for days on end, leaving the children to cope
alone. The father, an aggressive man, seems to have behaved
as though nothing untoward was occurring, leaving the
children to fend for themselves before leaving everyone for
good. The unrelieved nihilism the child faced produced an
oxymoronic state of mind in which imminent death was felt
to be a continual state, happening for random reasons. She
spoke of how she lived in such dread of her mother's death
that its 'actuality' somehow took hold of her. Certainty that
her mother was *about* to die widened into rumination over
when it would happen, which was always imminent. Inevitably, when her mother did die decades later at the age of 91
and of natural causes, my patient's terror of her imminent
death was so established that the mother's actual passing
had little impact. The mother remained on this tormenting
cusp of death long after her actual demise.

When my patient was unhappy with me she became silent
and the hum of terror grew louder, and when she wasn't it
was like an untreated virus of suspicion, affecting everything. Her speech was stilted and rehearsed, movements
hesitant unless predictable, vigilance unwavering, restful

sleep impossible. She helped me to see that she lived *within* death, fueled by her own hatred, and this picked the flesh off her bones. It reminded me of the Keres, the 'sisters' of Thanatos, who craved human blood. These spirits of violent or cruel death in battle, accident, disease or murder preyed upon the wounded and dying, tearing out their souls for consignment to Hades before devouring what remained. They themselves did not have the power to bring about death: they stalked the wounded like vultures, feeding once they died. My patient seemed to be picked at and torn apart by terror of death, her soul consigned to hell and her body ravaged by pain, but she was not allowed to die. I began to see that this infusion of death did not make her life futile but a life of infinite torture, of herself and others. She characterized the hum of terror as a current of electricity, later as a pistol held to her head, clicking every few seconds. These descriptions led me to wonder about the experience of living under a never-to-be-revoked death sentence.

What she referred to as a 'hum of terror' marked the affliction of disintegration when the inviolate, unknowable private self of my patient, with which communication was neither sought nor required, had been laid bare. The splintering of her irreducible integrity produced feelings of lifelong disfigurement, hatred of life and people and terror of death. The hidden, shame-filled nature of wholesale devastation of this kind is rarely discussed. In TV shows, a small child is kidnapped and held for 2 weeks whilst dread mounts, adults fearing and then concluding the worst. The basement or cave is discovered, the child is found alive and police inform distraught parents *'She has been found unharmed'*, to a flood of tears and relief. Unharmed? The girl has, in all likelihood, been destroyed by this terror. Imagine my patient's experience of being held hostage not for a week or two but for each minute and hour of each day for 17 years, hope for anything destroyed, her own hatred rampant and being shamed internally by cackling disdain. I don't think it an exaggeration to suggest that her reaction to engulfment by death is akin to 'death row syndrome', which can rob condemned prisoners of their sanity but sometimes of any interest in further stays of execution, so agonizing is the process of withstanding repeated loss of hope. Is their refusal to allow themselves to be threatened any further the one control they have left to protect the integrity of the authentic self?

What must a psychoanalyst do? The lesson in humility provided by my patient pointed to her need for me to fully *accept* her situation, not to try to change it. This reflected her own lifelong attempts to accept the unacceptable which she did not, could not, achieve alone. The most unacceptable fact of all was that no one had known of her true existence. Alienation like this flies in the face of the need for wholeness and completeness, so her first demand of me had to be that I accept her failure to accept the unacceptable. In the process, I too had to fail to accept the unacceptable because, like her, I had to feel that it is beyond human capability to accept. Only then might I begin to accept her. When this impossible work is done, it becomes at least possible for two people to stand *together* at the graveside of a murdered girl, in grief and tribulation. The hum of terror is not prepared for this.

4

feral

stock still bare still stare still ice-cold stare still no back

stare left stare right stare front up down side stare no

back stare. still stock still stare no back stare behind.

dark stare still light dark sky bare stare air still stare grass still

wet still stare can't stare no back stare behind. maybe fly. kill fly

dead still stare kill no fly no behind no stare behind no back stare

no behind still kill fly no fly. dark stare kill still no light no behind.

shite eat shite can't shite eat shite still stare kill no behind fly kill

fly stock still fly both not both stock still fly no off no on still no on

no off not both stare still kill behind still stare behind still can't no

back stare no behind stare right stare front up down stare still

dark eat shite no shite more dark still stare hold up entrails still

stare stop dark still.

DOI: 10.4324/9781003176862-4   27

5

STROKES OF FORTUNE

'Light griefs can speak: deep sorrows are dumb'.
Seneca in Montaigne: *Essays* (2009, p. 98)

It began when my French teacher (of *'all very modest dentists must not eat spinach after portions of rhubarb tart'* fame)[1] came up to me in the windy, stone corridor next to the classroom and said:

> *'What are you going to do when you leave school?'*
> *'Dunno'.*
> *'Would you like to go to Normandy in France and work as an assistant teacher of English in a school there?'*
> *'Okay'.*

That was that. I could not have anticipated such a stroke of fortune. It took 30 years to realize it wasn't good luck. I think he knew what he was doing and, if so, it was the kindest act anyone had shown me. In school I had learned nothing and was bullied. His proposal changed things, even before I got there. I had something to look forward to. I saved my wages as a bus conductor for a train ticket and flight in a WW2 transporter plane from Southampton to Cherbourg and a bus through the countryside of La Manche. The school was a small seminary in Coutances run by a community of priests in black vestments, nuns and lay teachers, with 200 or so children from 5 to 18. Imagine being airlifted by magic carpet from a desolate corner of Merseyside and lowered onto a Normandy meadow to the sound of bees, a church bell and the occasional cockerel. A stranger takes you to lunch with welcoming, calm people served food so unintelligibly delicious you don't know where to start or stop eating. Lunch was not something I knew about. You are shown to your room and told you need do nothing for a week except attend the three banquets a day. On top of this, they paid me. Though non-religious, I believe in miracles.

The impact of this civility could not enter my mind, degraded as it was to a survival mentality, so it entered my body. Two years were needed to accept the reality of delectable, natural food appearing each day. No one screamed or hit out. Silence denoted peace, not danger. Looking back, nothing happened, and this was the seminary's greatest virtue. The priests were committed to their vocation and went about teaching and mentoring in an unhurried way. The children seemed, to me, to be cooperative and not cowed. I was asked one morning to meet with the director of the seminary, Père Robine, who told me that the English teacher I worked with, Père Denis, had been admitted to hospital for surgery and asked if I would be willing to teach his class. He offered me Père Denis's salary, which was a great deal more than the allowance I was paid, so I said yes. I had never taken a class on my own before and tried my best, but the students tended to chatter, and I had difficulty controlling this. One day I became irritated and said abruptly:

'Taisez vos gueules.'

I did not know that the word *gueule* was used to describe the mouth of an animal and was a term of abuse when applied to people. In effect, I'd said *'Shut your ugly gobs'*. Inevitably it got back to parents, who complained to the seminary. I was mortified when Père Robine called me into his study to explain that such a term wasn't used between people. He wasn't mortified. He wasn't even angry or authoritarian. With hindsight I think he was explaining calmly something new to a hapless 17-year-old who, he knew, had never taught a class before, and it allowed me to return to the now wide-eyed class who stared at me like I was an animal in a zoo (I thought).

In those days women did cooking, and I discovered the kitchens next to the refectories where nuns kneaded dough for large loaves of bread *(gros pains)* which came out golden from the oven with an aroma that filled the whole world and on which floated breakfast conversation each morning. A massive carthorse arrived one morning pulling a trailer with high wicker sides. At the rear was a stone mill under which hung a bucket. The driver proceeded to each apple tree in the seminary's orchard, accompanied by local people who picked the apples and tossed them into the trailer. When it was full the stone mill crushed the apples to produce juice which became the cider we drank and which when distilled produced the regional *digestif*, 'Calvados', the fragrance of which was so alluring as to make me wary. I struggled when I saw local policemen on motorbikes and in police cars pull up in the early morning outside a *bar tabac* in the town square and ask for *café-calva* – espresso with a separate glass of Calvados and two cubes of sugar on the side. The sugar was dipped into the Calvados and the liqueur sucked between sips of coffee. It was a bit disgusting, to my prim mind, but that wasn't my worry. I pictured responsible policemen drunk in pileups all over the place.

I made friends with one or two other lay teachers and visited their homes. Whilst socially inept, I was interested in how different life was in this rural community compared to anything I'd known. Routines were earthbound, tied to seasons, days of the week, saints' holidays, Sunday after-noon walks, football and rugby matches, the annual Tour de France and, above all, meals. I was horrified that fami-lies bred rabbits in hutches and killed them blithely for the next meal, as they also did with chickens and geese. It was tormenting that meals were so delicious, but I rationalized that it wasn't cruelty because it was the same attitude to food that animals had. We have to eat so we have to kill. We're all animals. This did not resolve the experience of pleasure, which I did not know was my problem. Or that the country families treated animals well, fed them prop-erly and dispatched them swiftly. This killing was different from cruelty. How? It was decades before I could answer these questions.

I had one highly embarrassing experience in the seminary. I was a 17-year-old virgin who had not had a girlfriend. One evening I found Radio Caroline on my tran-sistor radio.[2] I wrote to them telling them I wanted to cor-respond with people, especially girls, and spelled out my situation. To my amazement, the seminary received many letters *daily* addressed to me, mostly from young women, a few gay men and some ladies of a certain age. I had gotten what I wished for. Priests and occasionally a nun would bring yet another bundle of mail to my room, and I would smile, speechless, offering no plausible explanation, trying to make light of it. Until I decided to tell the truth. To my surprise, no one was judgemental, except me. They were amused, I think, and their unflustered responses reminded me of how nothing happened in the seminary, which was its most reassuring quality.

Assaults of kindness on my senses were bewildering. I watched them wash over me. Years of mental dereliction could not be erased, but seepages of enlightenment from decent people took hold of my body and became a foothold for appetite and curiosity. Is this hope? By the time I left the seminary, I had experienced a feeling of satisfaction for the first time in my life – a feeling of having enough. Can such an ordinary notion capture a metamorphosis I am unable to forget?

Why I didn't stay in France is a question I have asked myself many times. I wish I had, but I think I lacked a feeling of entitlement to choose. I also had the idea I was English and so went back. Adrift on Merseyside, I saw two things. People needed money and a place to sleep. After a few menial jobs I hated I was told that advertising paid well. By a stroke of luck, I was taken on to train as a copywriter by a Manchester ad agency. Despite panic that I knew nothing and not sleeping for a week, my work was accepted and, to my surprise, I did well, reaching a senior position. At 22 I moved to a London agency and a year after that started my own company. No bosses and, incredibly, an income 10 times my previous salary. I knew never to work for anyone again. In the 1960s and early 1970s advertising flourished and I was inundated with campaigns, TV commercials, the works. I had a knack for it. I saved money with the idea of redoing my failed education and going to university. Advertising, though lucrative, was repetitive, largely mindless and tainted by excesses I found seductive and threatening. I cut back and began my re-education at a working man's college in Lambeth where I took the A Level exams required to enter university. I passed the exams but didn't believe the name on the letter for a month.

In those days there existed a prejudice against mature university students and it took 5 years of applying before I was offered a leftover place to study rats in the Psychology Department of University College London. I nearly didn't get the place after three tired lecturers started grilling me about whether or not I was serious about going to university and I lost my temper:

> *'I've applied each year for five years and am planning on giving up a lucrative job in advertising. If that isn't serious, how do YOU define serious!?'*

I resigned myself to never going to university. Fuck it. A letter of acceptance arrived a few days later. It taught me once more that anger is not always a destructive thing, a lesson I needed to learn repeatedly. I wanted to study anthropology and braced myself to ask for a transfer to the Anthropology Department if they would have me and, fortunately, the transfer was granted. Studying in a Marxist Anthropology department whilst still working in the moral swamp of advertising was stressful, to say the least, but I graduated and undertook a PhD at the Maudsley Psychiatric Hospital where I was befriending patients on locked wards.

There, I met Murray Jackson, Robert Cawley and Henri Rey. Jackson and Cawley ran a therapeutic milieu for personality-disordered and psychotic inpatients who stayed for a year or two, something unheard of today. Jackson's interviews with these individuals inspired me. Watching from behind a one-way screen, I was moved to see ordinary conversation emerge out of, what was to me, absolute chaos. An imperceptible changing of gears, a coaxing of sanity from desperate confusion, struck me as a thing of great beauty and pointed me in the direction of analytic training. Though alienated for my first 17 years, I had come to see the importance of beauty – a corrective to mental pain – which had contributed to saving me from insanity. The Woods, fresh-baked bread in France, the tranquility of the nuns and priests, an Alfa Romeo Spyder, my Vespa, the wind and sky, Jackson's skill, patients' courage.

I'd begun therapy before moving to London with a Jungian analyst in London's Harley Street, minutes' walking distance from Euston rail station. A Manchester rabbi I knew asked his analyst for the name of someone, and twice a week I undertook the 400-mile round trip from Manchester to London, occasionally in the lavatory to avoid the ticket inspector, and when I moved to London I increased my sessions to four. After my first session I hovered a few feet above the ground for days. The relief at being listened to was unlike anything I had experienced. The *space* felt like ambrosia; everything invasion wasn't. I took to missing sessions, putting work first, with no idea that I felt guilt at getting help, and he didn't bring it up save for postcards saying how sorry he was to not see me. Blowing hot and cold plagued my dealings with people. On the surface, beneath the surface, loss terrified me. I had homosexual dreams. My analyst didn't know what to do with them, so I quit. I tried others without success. One man sat on the far side of a wood-paneled room with stained glass windows intoning the numinous qualities of the unconscious.

A grand woman I went to see gave me a picture of the Shroud of Turin. Eventually, I came across someone as straight as a cricket bat. My taste of civilization had been the seminary, but not an individual. With this person I had the same dumbfounded feeling. His unruffled interest entered my body. An ancient mariner with a white beard, modest and kind, he possessed qualities I neither recognized nor understood. I could write a book about our 3 years together. He made one mistake. When he heard I'd been accepted into the analytic training he was delighted and supportive, including with their condition that I end with him and begin with a training analyst. He predicted great things. This is one thing I feel angry with him about, an unjustified anger because he almost certainly could not have dissuaded me from doing the training. I thought I had found the civilized family I was looking for. He might have at least warned me. What I had with him was, I now know, rare. In retrospect, he was the first man I loved.

The training analyst I saw for 7 years was famous, charismatic and firmly middle-class. She was creative, engaged and not without humor, which I appreciated. She did something helpful by insisting I delay the academic and clinical sides of the training in favor of 2 years of private analysis. I balked but with hindsight realize that she was right. She became preoccupied by what she saw as my 'resilience', a quality I didn't recognize or feel, and this gave rise to an unspoken dissonance between us, despite which I qualified and immersed myself in clinical work for a decade, during which I experienced a further stroke of great good fortune. I worked for 6 years editing *The International Journal of Psychoanalysis* with Glen Gabbard, a psychiatrist, analyst and remarkable individual who became a friend and brother.

Despite the efforts I had made to get help for myself, I still did not feel that I understood myself to my core or why fears and anxieties still tormented me in dreams and relationships. I dreaded not getting to the heart of this, fearing emotional isolation. There is an aftermath for children who live with neglect and invasion, beyond disturbance to their personalities. They cannot learn and do not know how things work. With little or no structure to time, days or nights, no understanding of thoughts or feelings and, crucially, no one to help negotiate the demands of living, they are at sea in the most basic way imaginable. An ordinary infant places one building block on top of another, the parent nods and communicates 'Yes, that's how it's done', and the next block is easier, and so on. This affiliation is missing. It is not a failure of cognition, which also fails due to isolation. When there is no one to help, confidence fails and imagination atrophies. It is tempting to think improvisation might be employed to get by (resilience?), but artfulness is out of reach for such children, who instead *guess* at reality. Using primitive fantasies they devise high-risk guessing strategies that substitute for development. The child mutates into a quasi-adult and yet is neither.

The long-term outcome of this atrophy is a failed imagination which shows itself as fear of people and life and is unaltered by any amount of adaptation, education or achievement. The child has struggled in the physical world without a functioning mind, employing willpower and delusion to fight isolation and futility. Until awakening of imagination becomes possible, nothing can change, and change is something that cannot occur alone.

Statements like *'I discovered who I was in analysis'* or *'I came alive'* or *'I no longer feel like an outsider'* echo a birth of imagination alongside and through the imagination of another. Statements like *'I learned a great deal in my analysis'* point to failure, in my view. Analysis is about experiencing, not studying or learning. Connection through affiliation enables the individual to create a life (and eventually a death) of their own, attachment of imaginations and selves having been constituted. Fear of life is born of an absence of people and loss of imagination.

I heard that the ancient mariner had been admitted to hospital with a life-threatening cancer. We had kept in touch, so I visited him. Seeing him incapacitated was incongruous and upsetting. Eventually, he conquered his illness and was due to be discharged when I was told he had contracted a hospital infection. I went that evening and was shocked to see him looking gaunt and weak. We talked, but he was tired. As I left, he took my hand and said, *'I love you'*. Speechless, I found myself saying *'I love you'*. It was the last time I saw him. It was the first time a man had told me he loved me.

I had done the rounds of analysts enough to know that my last shot needed to be decisive. Either I got what I needed or I quit. The analytic training, now long behind me, meant I could set the conditions. I found someone and told him I was deadly serious – if he screwed up, I'd fire him. No concessions. I had the space and privacy to say what I liked and did. What transpired is conveyed in *The Fifth Principle* (Williams, 2010). This final analysis taught me three qualities needed in a genuine analyst: patience, honesty and kindness – in other words, intelligence. Cleverness is not intelligence. Joseph Sandler was fond of saying, *'Analysis is about making friends with parts of ourselves we don't like'* (personal communication). How can this be done without patience, honesty and kindness? I can't recall these qualities being mentioned, let alone discussed, during my training. Another discovery I made was that unless we experience our own psychosis, it isn't an analysis worthy of the name.

I began painting what turned out to be a larger canvas than I had anticipated, with no knowledge of what would appear. Were an observer to have eavesdropped on the sessions, they might have concluded we were both insane, honesty being what it is. Without honesty, I would have wasted the time I had left. Letting go of self-reliance produced more shame, rage and grief than I had anticipated but, for some reason, no need to prostrate myself.

As the canvas took shape, I began to experience compassion at what I saw. It entered my body, as before, but feelings also began to emerge for the child in me and for what my late sister and my surviving sister had experienced. The birth of my own children and their development were critical, often leaving me dumbstruck with wonder. A thought entered my mind during this final analysis that I could see I would be never be able to shake. To lead a life of integrity I needed to accept myself fully and completely for who I was. Obvious, perhaps, but not to me. Sandler had been right. The isolation, deaths, misery, intelligence, anger, grief, love – all of it called for acceptance if I were to be reconciled with myself. Capitulation or passivity were unnecessary, because the facts spoke for themselves. If I could not accept them, I could not accept myself to my core. The most difficult acceptance of all was of good qualities I possessed.

The canvas assumed a life of its own and introduced me to a new-found respect for my body, previously a survival machine, and its ability to care for the mind in times of disaster. Living with the sadnesses of the past no longer entailed depression. The experience of genuine trust, something that is far more difficult to achieve than is commonly imagined, opened the door to a capacity to say Yes and No and to mean it. And to fall in love.

Notes

1 This sentence was invented by him to help recall French verbs that take *etre* in the past tense rather than *aller*. They are *Aller, Venir, Monter, Descendre, Mourir, Naitre, Entrer, Sortir, Arriver, Partir, Rester, Tomber*.

2 Radio Caroline was a pop music radio station founded in 1964 by Ronan O'Rahilly to circumvent broadcasting regulations in the UK and Europe that were controlled by major record labels. He leased a ship, moored it in the English Channel and broadcast non-stop popular music, launching the careers of many subsequently well-known disc jockeys.

6

GONE

When you die at a young age, strange things happen.

Most are out of reach but the strangest and most paradoxical of them is being unaware that it has happened whilst at the same time experiencing it each moment.

This could be thought of as 'Gone'.

Not Gone temporarily or in search of an alternative but Gone never to return.

There may be different ways Gone can come about, like infant suicide or the crushing of a soul, but whatever form it takes, two things need to occur at the same time.

One is being unoccupied or uninhabited. There is no one, inside or out, to see what is taking place. The second is an experience of inner violence so intense as to give rise to a paralyzing of imagination.

I am uninhabited, I am inundated.

This is not the same as psychosis, though this may ensue. Gone exists prior to psychosis and denotes a loss of life at its core.

DOI: 10.4324/9781003176862-6

Absence of interest in the Gone child concentrates subjective experience in bodily action. Nothing is what it seems, a lack of comprehension so sweeping that objects are reified as either inscrutable or threatening.

A tree is harmless until it rains, a bus a dog-fight pit, car an intergalactic missile, body a machine, shit a shocking punishment, food a conspiracy, sky sheet metal and so on.

Misrecognition on this scale prevents learning, a deficit felt bodily, the body of an automaton, not a deficit taken in mentally, because the learning process has not been learned.

I know what I already knew – physical pandemonium.

The world of Gone is raw, outside space and time, consisting of upheaval frozen in the nothing it represents.

Indifference, the precursor to Gone, is a vacuum force unlike anything else.

From nowhere, indifference activates a gravitational vortex that whips craving into a planetary cyclone, like Jupiter's Great Red Spot.[1]

Predicated on the actuality of nothing, indifference views as axiomatic the destruction of everything that is not itself.

Without prescience of something that anything else might be the scheme could miscarry, so an equation *everything - not everything - nothing* dismantles the problem of everything and its loss at its inception, in the needs of an infant.

The effect of indifference might seem akin to neglect, but neglect fails in its lethargic unconcern to convey the resolve needed to achieve indifference.

Annihilation of need requires doggedness and ingenuity.

The outcome, for both parties, is barrenness scarred by vestiges of butchery, a landscape beyond neglect.

Indifference renders me the last remaining life form of a desecrated land.

The Gone child, unable to know anything, cannot learn or change. Some may learn something from experience, but if the learning apparatus is stillborn, adaptation is the sole option, there being no one available to learn anything.

From the basic facts of life – birth, development and death – to the stuff of life between is a closed book to the Gone child who adopts the least harrowing stance – indifference.

A swell of grievance or pining indicating hope that Gone need not be forever propels Gone's chilling tide of apathy to drown what remains.

Indifference is not the prerogative of the ill. Parents, schoolteachers, public servants, clerics, young people – all of us can display indifference if truth proves to be indigestible.

This encourages further concealment by the Gone child.

Consider the discernment and prudence needed to identify, let alone engage with, Gone.

Everything has Gone.

The residual nothingness before you that passes for a life form could stand for anything, from shy or withdrawn to woebegone, depraved or insane, depending upon its ramshackle presentation.

Who cares anyway? The Gone child walks, turns up, leaves, goes 'home', day after day, week after week, doesn't it? What is there to say?

A Gone child makes imperceptible yet overwhelming demands, is unmanageable and is disappeared.

Insensibility is their first order of business. Any communication is on the lines of: *'Gone. Desperate. Return under no circumstances. Stop'*.

Rules of engagement of a rational kind run aground immediately.

The only thing, the dreadful thing, that offers a hope of correspondence lies in *our* willingness to experience what it is like to feel Gone.

The Gone condition, founded upon absolute mistrust, takes nothing for granted: no analyst, authority, talk, gesture.

It fumbles helplessly for some unidentified, putative ally who will suspend belief, tolerate disarray, suffer incongruous, unjustified assaults, breathe a toxic, confounding fog and be willing to suffer an experience of ruination.

Small wonder Gone people are inconspicuous and loath to elicit concern.

Smaller wonder still they deter the mental health profession.

The Gone individual anticipates ostracism and neither you nor I grasp the sheer number of ways in which this is inflicted. We have to be taught.

Whatever shape the induction takes, it is a *rite de passage* not to be confused with torture, despite the resemblances. The injunction is that we be taken out of ourselves in a way not previously experienced and traverse the path of Gone at as many intersection points as we can bear.

Mercifully, the Gone individual cannot tolerate exposure for long, so the process is paced and cyclical.

I/she/he need infinite space and time to formulate a second communication: *'Gone. Desperate. Return under no circumstances. Stop. Go'.*

I dread my susceptibility to this hubris, kindling of spent ashes, but I ask you for help anyway, an unthinkable idea, and you accede. Delusional.

Dismay at your many presumptions plunges me into insentience. You are insane. Is anything real? Am I alive? Dead? Dead whilst breathing?

In trying to negotiate in bare feet ice pinnacles and gales, crossroads and so-called meeting points, I throw a sidelong glance in acknowledgement, in the certainty that you will die, suddenly or little by little, as you mistakenly accept, and fail to mistakenly accept, desecration that befouls and pauperizes.

For me, torture, stabbing, terror. For you, vexation, degeneracy, impotence.

The doomed folly cannot go on. Goes on. I kill, you suffer, I kill. To what end?

Perhaps a difference between this lunacy and Gone might be I am not Gone.

Meeting points, of which I have no knowledge, contravene Gone.

I do not seek friendship or understanding. These ideas appall me. I do not know who you are, who anyone is. I don't want to know. Or to not know. I don't want.

I need you to accept only that I am Gone. I don't know I need this, so I don't know you know or don't know I need this and don't know.

No guidance, instruction, help. Just pinnacles, gales, crossing points, menace.

I fear, hate, cower, abscond but do not know I misread.

I do not know that you know or do not know that I misread and do not know.

Filth, stigma, misery. The light drip of acceptance unfelt. Your frustration, resentment, boredom, indifference are proof you do not, cannot, care. You cannot suffer such calumny: no one can, other than me.

What is the point? Tantalizing inferences at crossroads you will recite for years unless I put a stop to it.

At one intersection a mighty collision triggers a multiple pileup. Smoke, flames, burning wrecks. I run for my life but before I can get away I am questioned by police and paramedics about what happened. Outraged, I fucking tell them what happened. No charges are pressed. I am lucky to be alive. Thanks a lot.

You?

A drawn-out inquest investigates the death of a child, a serious matter, so every detail has to be Gone through.

Meanwhile, more crossing points, near misses, no smashes, for now.

Why on earth risk it again? I appear to have had to change direction, or driving style, or something as I see the problem lies not just with my annihilation but in making you see that you are, I now know, out of your mind.

And so on.

At intersections divergent realities collide, never in exactly the same way, instigating a thousand different outcomes, loud, soft, dark, bright, great, small, imperceptible. I see some but not others.

My body returns unbidden.

Points of intersection, terrifying, shameful, enraging, accrue, yet beckon my body and me (?) to accept you (?) are there, I (?) am there and accept you (?) accept I (?) am there.

This is unwelcome. To think you (?) know me (?), accept me (?), incenses me.

I can negotiate crossroads. I can appear to listen. I know what works. Work.

In Gone there is only work, work to stave off death. What worked works. My body may turn up, but I work.

I am sickened that shame and fear dominate my life, whatever that is.

Let me put this candidly. I have no interest in what you say.

A holding pattern is needed to put what I know to better use.

Realism.

The holding pattern, too close to Gone, does not silence dreams of being lost and abominated.

You notice with your usual contrivances, feeble surmises, my body insolently returns. I do not accept this.

Must I endure more nothing when I know nothing works?

Did I not accept this?

Why did you accept this when you had a job to do?

I am to accept this?

Accept me? Accept you? Accept nothing I accept?

Dreams. Defeat, appalling decisions, a thousand forfeited opportunities, longings, grief.

The themes repeat themselves, crisscrossing each other.

Did you know this?

I no longer see which theme is which, not that I ever could. Did you?

Crisscrossing? Crossing Points? Crossroads?

Am I missing something?

I talked about this, didn't I? I'm sure I did.

Did you hear?

You replied.

Was this me (?) speaking, you (?) listening?

You (?) speaking, me (?) listening?

What were the thousand intersections?

A thousand lost opportunities?

A thousand lethal injections?

Neither?

Were you (?) there?

You (?) accepted them?

Accepted me (?)?

You (?) present?

Me (?) present?

You (?) accept me (?)

Gone?

Note

1 A spinning, anticyclonic storm twice the size of Earth, believed to have existed for at least 350 years, producing wind speeds of 425 mph and temperatures of 2420°F. Different, freezing variations surround Saturn with winds of 1,500 mph and temperatures of −280°F.

7

SHAME

'Much Madness is divinest Sense –
To a discerning Eye –
Much Sense – the starkest Madness –
'Tis the Majority
In this, as All, prevail –
Assent – and you are sane –
Demur – you're straightaway dangerous –
And handled with a Chain –'

Emily Dickinson (Johnson, 1961, p. 435)

I feel shame and love disappears.

I have no way to conceal my fall from grace, which leaves everyone in no doubt I am beyond redemption. What makes it unlike anything else is its pervasiveness, no matter how long or short, that robs me, in public, of any right to compassion, so colossal is my failure. I want 'the floor to open up', to 'disappear', to 'die of shame', cementing shame's affinity with death. Barely remitting shame obscures shattered self-esteem and may proffer suicide in the hand of friendship, hope for viability gone despite my efforts at salvage. Exclusion and moral condemnation are the internal and external conditions for shame. In gangrene

DOI: 10.4324/9781003176862-7

or necrotic mortification, a part of the body dies whilst the rest remains alive. In shame, death radiates from the core.

How did I become so ashamed? Tricks of the mind? Cruelty? I feel violence. Screaming – No!! Wailing, shriveled, a stupefied dot. Anything but screaming. I must get my 'mind' around the fact that this is the end and I am the one who caused it. My attempts to get what I needed were unnatural and cruel, the consequences ruinous, yet they were nothing compared to my treachery. At once a pariah and slovenly ghost, sunk in shame, no mind, body, name, soul, home, I tinker with trappings strewn across the path, under reproof that I, with no self, am and always was inconceivable. Tantalized by the lure of nothing I take to be something, I slip into a sea of glass shards, motion my salve.

Excess shame makes it public there is nobody in the world willing to show me love. They stare in abhorrence. Opprobrium foments humiliation at having fallen so far below accepted standards, but it is the disbarring of redemption that kills. The final reckoning, delirium forebodes, is a diaspora of one, rotted, forsaken. There lies the authority of shame, not its aim. Shame does not murder. Despite itself, it struggles pathetically for connection. It is condemnation by exclusion and purgation that murders. My collusion with their proclamation that shame is justified is critical to acceptance of my annihilation.

Humiliation, shame's attack dog, importunes with a promissory note. If I only agree with their horror-struck estimations, reprieve from disgrace can follow. Admit to having betrayed values that are mandatory is all that it takes. No thinking required. Accede, yes, with a certain amount of self-hatred, but then all is forgiven. I succumb, my soul blackened. If ever I were intelligent, I am no longer. Borges wrote: '. . . *my father was a very intelligent man, and like all intelligent men he was very kind'* (Borges, 1970, pp. 206–207). Without kindness, there can be no intelligence. Autocrats and clairvoyants, believing in their intelligence, profit from credulity shamed, warping expiation and the promise of re-inclusion into capitulation and despotism. I cede to this deceit, a vagrant indebted to the slavery that saves me.

The truth of shame is that I have been disappeared. I know it yet do not know it. The withdrawal of love that unmasks me as irredeemable means I may no longer show my face. Wormwood infests me with guilt that is real. This guilt is manipulated by dictators, power mongers, class systems and the self-serving to shackle the disgraced.[1] Its bitter pill, when swallowed whole, leads to lifelong, futile attempts at reparation or perhaps doing the honorable thing. I convinced myself I had succeeded and was proved wrong, failing for reasons I do not understand but which inverted my world. In confusion, with no capacity to think, my passing is sealed by a black hole.

Guilt can make other emotions pale in significance. It annuls intimacy and eviscerates life. If shame ruins, guilt kills because *everything* is my fault. Clemency is out of reach, because pleading rouses public scrutiny, intensifying shame and then guilt. What is left? Die, as many do or by chance note out of the corner of one eye that shame, reliant upon concealment of vileness, maintains that my failure is not yet public, whilst claiming it already is. Am I pretending it hasn't happened? That the worst is yet to come, when it has? Have I, like my overseers, become clairvoyant? A catastrophe killed me, leaving me helpless. I clasped at some imaginary skirt tails for dear life. Dead, surely I can't afford to die again? Shame and guilt prevent extinction, don't they? *Postmortem* I predict shame at being shamed, guilt at being found guilty, death at being dead, *ad nauseam*. Not just dead. Brainwashed.

When shame and guilt are welded together using cruelty, with no recognition of any good in the individual, there arises perverse excoriation and eternal death. I know I have died but continue to fiddle with clairvoyance, *bricolage*, knowing I am dead and not dead. Dead is dead. Not dead is not alive but death hereafter. Shamed to death yet subsisting. Dead yet radioactive. Is radioactivity proof of life (and death) after death? Everything I touch or see dies of radiation.[2] Radioactivity caused by disintegration of atoms, my atoms, then your atoms. A killer who killed his own and everyone else's atoms. A radioactive killer. My radioactivity is murder gone off the rails. Murder on the rails would be murder of my radioactive killers.

The greatest obstacle a shamed-to-death person faces lies in making the experience public, permanently and transparently, with no admission charge, like a good museum. We believe our shame to be already public, but we also don't believe it is. How can fear of inverting the inverted world be greater than what has already happened? It is and was for me. I was plagued by nightmares that I had murdered people, serial killer style, and had buried the bodies in roads under asphalt or in concrete bridge pillars so effectively they would never be found. Word got out that the police were hunting the killer. I became frantic that I had left marks on the roads and pillars that could expose my depraved enterprise. I confided in a friend that I was going mad with the nightmares. My friend had the novel idea of going to each murder site, digging up the bodies and laying them out for all to see. I would be present, emboldening people to take a good, long look so as to not miss any details. Wounds, bones, decaying flesh, lice, stench. If they turned away, I'd offer encouragement:

'I don't think it's a good idea to leave before seeing <u>this</u>. You really do need to see everything'

No square inch would be left concealed. Inevitably, the police would do what police do, but nothing they or anyone could do was worse than the insanity into which I was descending. Following this excavation work the nightmares began to fade and, for reasons that were never explained, the police wound down their investigations.

I kept myself locked in shame, no one else. Nothing I had done in my life could justify my shame and guilt. My friend stood by as I disclosed each transgression for what it was in a nonviolent but murderous revolt that took audacity, blind faith and help from someone with their eyes open. Public demonstrations like this unmask the goal of excess shame – exclusion and isolation – in its profligacy. There are today many people who are less intimidated by shame and guilt and who reject the abuse of psychological forces that fuels them. Honesty about origins, class, accent, oppression, conflicts, hopes and fears helps safeguard integrity from shame. Abused women and men speak out, whistleblowers are heard, priests seek redemption. Openness engenders both respect and opposition, but its impact lies in being a countermeasure to illusion and delusion by dismantling propaganda that barricades me from life and myself. Perhaps shame can never be entirely dispelled because it is a part of me, of who we all are. In the meantime, I can use openness and constructive hate to temper its greed for excess. Without shame and guilt, I feel connected, less impeded. I take you in, give you me, am inhabited by you, in conversation with you, awake or asleep. Power has no place in this.

Is shame a trauma? Is there 'ordinary' shame? Universality seems to be one of its qualities, so there must be multiple contexts in which it can arise. We hear a lot about Oedipal guilt but less about Oedipal shame, a more serious ruination of the self. Oedipus, unwanted and threatened with death, acts out his triumph, the consequences of which reflect not only his guilt but shame at the exposure of his early obliteration. There is nothing ordinary about this. In highly dysfunctional families where confusion, failings, catastrophic losses, emotional violence and perversity go ignored, dissembling, humiliation and alienation create toxic shame. In less dysfunctional families, loss of esteem in conflicts, rivalries, misjudgements and unspoken discordances generate shame. What both groups share, to differing degrees, is shame's excruciating pain. This experience may well be traumatic. Where the two groups diverge lies in their access to mourning. This is an irony of shame. It contains hope for redemption and reconnection. But if we drown in the shame of excommunication, fear-ridden, delusional battles with inner aggressors and killers prevent any appraisal of meaning, responsibility or lamentation for what has been lost, allowing shame and guilt to finish us off. Help will then stir hope and agony. Yet without help, an adult will be laid waste, a dead or dying infant disremembered.

The special category of the shameless and those who specialize in inflicting shame needs to be approached with trepidation, because the barbarism involved can blind the investigator. Expunged from human connection, soul slain, shamelessness launders desire into thrills of extermination, feeding off the destruction of those with ordinary human needs. For the shameless, hope is suicidal, their lives being as disposable as those they obliterate with relish.

Notes

1 Fascism, an ideology, is in fact a mechanism for purgation, its ultimate aim.
2 A survivor of the Warsaw Ghetto conveyed the loss of his humanity thus: 'If you could lick my heart, it would poison you'. (Claude Lanzmann (1985) *Shoah*).

8

PACTS

There is a type of relating that is widespread and compelling to the extent that it is accepted as a part of normal life and which can lure individuals into codependency of varying intensities and forms, frequently unbeknown to the participants. It gives rise to unhappiness that is insufficiently miserable to be relinquished in favor of something better. Tolerance of frustration and a seeming inability to overcome it derive from irrational but real fears of catastrophic loss, feelings that control and elude those involved. These fears are chronic. Efforts to overcome dread of being left may take the form of excited, imaginary triumphs over a never-ending crisis. Such victories of the imagination have the effect of reducing the incentive to forsake ways of relating that are self-destructive. Orgasmic gratification born of conquest without affection may, by employing a delusional premise, act as a substitute for a satisfying relationship. A pact is created by both parties who agree tacitly to be triumphed over in return for an undeclared covenant to never part.

Sadomasochism was the clinical term introduced in the late 19th century to describe a form of exciting sadistic

DOI: 10.4324/9781003176862-8

behavior that offers a channel for the expression of aggression in conditions of pseudo-safety. The term echoed the writings of Marquis de Sade (2016). This and other terms referring to manifestations of sexual deviance became grouped under the heading of perversions and were subject to moral condemnation, opprobrium and contempt. With time, associations to reprehensible sinfulness gave way to somewhat less value-laden terms such as 'sexual aberrations' or 'paraphilias'. Whilst sinfulness was a judgement based on religious and cultural values of limited explanatory weight, the notion of a vital need to transgress, including sexually, as an emotional imperative, received less attention. The sexual component of these pacts led to investigations of distinctions between affectionate love, sexuality and aggressive sexual conquests. In the latter – aggressive sexual conquests – affection appears to have a limited, if nonexistent role, the subject seeing and treating the object in a dehumanized form. On closer examination, the triumphs need not always be physical sexual acts, their psychic equivalent assuming precedence. The motivation for these activities is not always clear and remains today clouded by value judgements.

A Silicon Valley banker in his 50s sought help because he made relationships with troubled women who frustrated him terribly but whom he could not leave. Two marriages and divorces later, the latter initiated by the wives, he fell in love with a woman who, he says, criticizes everyone, especially him. Although the divorces had 'resolved' his dilemmas, he could not understand why he had used infinite reasonableness and appeasement to try to prevent the divorces from being finalized or the scale of relief he felt at finally being free of these women. His recent romance led to a third marriage. He loves his wife but her behavior, he states, is entirely irrational. She can be friendly, overly friendly even, only to find fault, become angry and alienate people. He beseeches and pleads with her to get her to see what she is doing, to no avail. A risk-taking habit he has had from adolescence – driving fast cars – has intensified with these stresses, leading to him driving thousands of miles over several days and nights to the point of exhaustion. What struck me when we met was the intensity and sincerity of his belief that he plays no part whatsoever in the conflicts. His intentions are solely reparative. The need to remain an innocent victim of misplaced animosity was more important than any specific crisis he described.

I was impeded from getting to know him by his talking more or less nonstop. It was a mixture of 'data' presented as evidence and moralizing judgements of his wife and others. His own feelings were missing, and nothing much I said changed this. His efforts to control me and the sessions were so determined and laborious that I was led to do something I had not done before. One day I got out of my chair, walked to the side of the couch and waved. I said:

'I need to interrupt you to ask you if you could slow down a little. The amount you are telling me is too much for my mind to take in'.

Unfazed, he slowed for about 10 minutes before resuming his rapid-fire monologue. What followed this enactment was that I became aware of something I had not grasped during the verbal onslaughts, which was his arousal as he built his case for the prosecution. Sessions might begin with a tiff about someone, usually his wife or a business colleague, which was being diplomatically handled by my patient until he felt justice wasn't prevailing. Thwarted demands (never voiced) for an apology (never forthcoming) led to frustration and mounting, pleasurable excitement. Comments I made were experienced as my inability to appreciate the unfairness of it all and were politely crushed. Meanwhile, life outside the sessions appeared to improve, with occasional accounts of business successes and allusions to passionate lovemaking with his wife. If I were to mention the word *sex* he would correct me sharply, insisting that for him it was 'lovemaking'. I felt steamrollered by his monologues, impotent and excluded. Eventually, I realized I felt like killing him. I knew from harrowing accounts that his father had been a violent, self-aggrandizing bully who had beaten his son and that his mother, by all accounts a brittle, capricious woman who had lost her own mother at an early age, did her best but failed to protect him. Instead, she sought emotional support from her son. His sister, an athletic girl 9 years older and much bigger than him, seems to have made it an imperative to taunt and humiliate him physically and emotionally. At the start of one session, aware of how much unacknowledged rage he was carrying, I asked him to sit in the chair and said:

> *'I want to let you know that I believe you have told me about terrible, humiliating things that have happened to you in your life. Perhaps you felt you might die. I think you are utterly outraged and furious as a result'.*

I was conscious of the risk involved in my bluntness but felt I had little choice. He was stunned by what I said and incredulous. The monologues resumed. Over time, he became more litigious in business conflicts and concerned at what he described as his wife's escalating outbursts, worrying that she might be mentally ill. Placating her and withdrawing, followed by high-speed car trips, became a pattern. He began an affair with a work colleague and found the sex exciting but when she pressured him to leave his wife, to the point of threatening to tell her of the affair, he had her quietly removed with a compensation payment and a signed order to remain silent. His appetite for affairs did not stop and he seduced several women, usually far from home, whilst being frightened that his wife would discover the infidelity. He ended affairs by withdrawing and neglecting the women in stages until they lost hope, all the while offering abject apologies. It became apparent that losing his wife and the affections of their teenage son was his primary fear, so he stopped the affairs but not before his wife found out about one of them and threatened to divorce him. Thrown into a panic he did everything he could to prevent this. His wife sought therapeutic help to deal with the crisis and became more frank with him. Disarmed, he provoked her increasingly, causing outbursts for which he blamed her before defusing these, fearing she would leave him. Intensive placations culminated in what he referred to as 'beautiful lovemaking'.

The sequence of provocation, sexual excitement, appeasement, withdrawal and relief seemed entrenched, and I said so in straightforward ways. The emotional deprivation he had experienced in his life made words difficult to feel. Increasing self-destructive behavior gave them more believability. He found himself in trouble with the board of his bank, having made appointments of people he had lionized only to find one was incompetent and another deceitful. He made investments with a hedge fund manager who committed fraud. Examples of poor judgement were no longer mere ideas to dismiss. The urge to seduce and

provoke continued but was modified by his wife's growing honesty, which he could not refute, and my efforts to
delineate the constraints on his thinking, despite his belief
that he was independent. The litany of his beleaguered
relationships became clearer to him, producing anxiety and
nightmares. He had barely spoken about his sister save for
her cruelty. The nightmares brought back incidents he had
forgotten, notably her pinning him down as a small child,
sitting on him and throttling him until his eyes bulged. In
one dream he wanted to fight back but was paralyzed. He
recalled neither parent doing anything to stop her despite
pleading with his mother. The father and daughter got on
well, he said. His father's cruelty had been terrifying but
less than his sister's because he knew the father's yelling
and beating would end. He believed that his sister did not
know when to stop. Memories of his parents' collusion led
to an awareness of his isolation and despairing peacekeep-
ing. As a child he followed his mother around listening to
her complaints, from which he 'learned how to manage' her
and the family. He was 'very close' to his mother, who confided in him about her unhappy childhood and marriage.

He developed chest pains and, worried about his chain
smoking and drinking, had himself hospitalized, and cardi-
ologists found him to be healthy. Extensive work on his illu-
sory powers of persuasion and misjudgement of others led
him to try to rein in his provocations. Somber, depression-
like states of hopelessness disguised a rage that was unfamiliar to him. His anger with his father and sister became
evident. His mother was a more confusing figure. 'Close-
ness' as her confidante had led him to devise strategies for
improving her moods using compliance and flattery, from
which he extracted appreciation. He was good at doing this,
he said. She would 'forget herself', laugh and joke at his

humor, responding with praise of his intelligence. From the age of 5 or so, they were a couple. The fury he harbored against his father and sister had a singular quality: he was outraged and wanted to destroy his bullies. Disentangling the seductive pact with his mother produced dismay and a sense of betrayal. He had believed that he lay at the center of his mother's life. The dance the two of them performed to distract themselves from their miseries and family crises struck him as horrifyingly degenerate until he came to see that she was the centre of *his* life and without her, he was convinced he would die. Their dance was a sacrificial act. He had 'agreed' to minister to his mother in return for the exciting, 'special' mothering she provided. Her motives, less clear, may have included a pursuit of mothering and comfort from him. It was, it seemed, a mutual sacrifice.

In adult life he seduced women, usually unhappily married women, by fervently attending to their needs until, the conquest made, he felt trapped by their demands, which he placated excitedly whilst feeling unable to leave. The parallels with childhood were not lost on him. He had desperately needed his mother, had to separate from her if he was to grow up, but was required to take care of her, surrendering his development for the thrill of being 'the love of her life', which took the place of genuine mothering. Betrayal tainted both lives. The women he seduced were cast in the same mold. He fell in love with the idea of a perfect union: mutual admiration and blissful compatibility. The fly in the ointment was the woman's troubled personality. This discovery startled him each time. The need for him to extinguish disagreements, seen as harbingers of dangerous loss, was irresistible. As he talked about these women, the discrepancy between the imaginary partner and the actual person was stark. The former would care for and protect him, soothe his agitated mind and submit willingly and excitedly to his sexual advances. Submission by persuasion was the aspect that gave him most satisfaction because it gave rise to an 'eternal peace' that descended on him. By contrast, the person he had to 'manage' was insatiably demanding, self-preoccupied and blind to appreciating how hard he worked to satisfy her. To prevent her from leaving, and to stop himself from leaving her, he threw himself into 'understanding' her problems until, propitiated, she simmered down and yielded to him. Exhausted, he would take himself off on high-speed drives to gain some respite.

The ideal woman installed in his mind was static and unchanging, an ageless goddess, lively, smiling and interested in only one thing – reaching orgasm with him. At one point he told me that the woman was in need of experiencing an incessant orgasm, which he was invited to maintain. Continuous orgasming as a form of pain medication was an idea he could not accept. He felt I was exaggerating, trying to take his very life source from him. He likened his ministrations to demanding women as 'half-assed psychiatric management' he couldn't resist but a price worth paying for the reward. I thought the preservation of the perfect woman who desired *him* was a life-or-death matter. His high-speed car driving courted extreme danger of falling into the arms of death, like the arms of this perfect woman, open to receive and devour him. The sacrificial commitment to 'helping' these women seemed to have no limit, which is understandable given what was at stake. Without a radical strategy he probably could not have survived his family of origin without going insane, and his mother was his lifeline. To get what he needed from her he was prepared to offer his own life. This may be what is commonly referred to as masochism, but the term leaves out the depth of primary devotion to another person that transcends the lure of death and without which life is impossible to live. There is a terrible heroism in this act which goes unnoticed.

The *idee-fixe* of the perfect woman I took to be a hallucination deriving from a very early fantasy of his mother he could not forsake. Each woman was slotted into his vision of a heavenly Madonna until things went wrong. Sweetened by seduction, they were required to be punished and rehabilitated, his anger with them being too dangerous to feel, let alone expose. Internal restoration of the orgasming Madonna was the imperative. The two diametrically opposed versions of a woman needed to constitute this kind of relating, versions which are experienced as completely irreconcilable, despite apparent efforts to the contrary, reflect a violent division in a subject faced with drastic early failure in connection, a gulf that feels impossible to bridge and which threatens death. His passionate fabrication of the desired and desiring, iconic Madonna is not only a salve against mental pain. It is a defense against suicide, her hallucination a last-resort, psychotic act.

9

FUCK IT

One way to think about schizophrenia (a questionable and, to my mind, moribund term) is a pounding of the mind and personality by alternating seductions and intimidations that are felt to be real. It is an oppression that places the incommunicado authentic self in mortal danger through exposure. The undermining of the subject's agency is drastic, so that moment-to-moment survival in a menacing world is a dominant preoccupation. Seductions from a fantastical world promise relief from all pain and confusion. Power is deemed ultimately to be external to the subject, including in auditory and visual hallucinations, and is countered by delusional methods of avoidance and withdrawal. Ordinary methods of engagement, in which subject and object carry equal authority, untrammeled by lack of respect, are unavailable having been deposed by processes of invasion. Violation of sanity and unendurable exposure of the authentic self have occurred. Without adequate protection to deal with the psychosis, recovery is unlikely and the grave threat to the authentic self will persist.

Protection from psychosis requires, above all, an ally to help identify psychotic invasions, their origins, aims and

DOI: 10.4324/9781003176862-9

consequences. An ally being unthinkable, at first this may need to be a witness, befriender, bystander or guest. If a rudimentary conversation is allowed to take place about the subject's experience, nonpsychotic moments of exchange may act as seeds of sanity, some of which could germinate. Of course, an ally may remain unthinkable, perhaps for years, and discussion of the necessity for and unobtainability of such an ally, seemingly nowhere to be seen, may be the focus of attention, but this is fine. What is taking place in this tentative alliance is the gradual construction of a triangle of inestimable value, without which no mind can function.

One corner of the triangle is the psychosis. Committed to a single, overarching endeavor, the psychosis advises, seduces, manipulates, menaces, perverts and, if necessary, terrorizes the nonpsychotic thinking of the individual into relinquishing the idea that connection with another human being might be of benefit. Conceiving of itself as protector of the subject's best interests, a belief with ties to disturbing experiences in infancy, the psychosis sets about weaving contradictory, irrational, compelling arguments for withdrawal and stasis by appealing to and exploiting the subject's fears and vulnerabilities. It does this over a prolonged period until a cult-like belief system is installed. Escalating, seductive persuasions vary in intensity depending on the extent to which the individual is in active need of help from another person. The psychosis will intensify or soft-pedal its activity according to the scale of digression from the imperative of radical isolation, but its underlying proscriptive task remains continuous and without interruption. No nontrivial human contact is advised or permitted and reliance upon the internal psychotic narrative is held to be mandatory.

A highly organized form of terror may be constructed from an assemblage of the individual's particular and immediate fears. For example, if a person is deeply afraid of aggression, their own and everyone else's, destructive anger may have established itself within the psychosis. Moment-to-moment instances of actual or potential aggression, usually in fantasy, are evoked, seized upon and exaggerated by the psychosis to convince the individual that catastrophic, violent conflict is imminent. These repetitive disaster threats, usually imaginary (there being no difference between reality and the imaginary) can attain such thematic salience as to seal off any frontier or backwater that might offer sanctuary. Time and space are distorted to stand for infinite sameness in support of macro and micro levels of threat that disorientate and imprison the subject's mind. In schizophrenia, fears of aggression, disintegration and total loss are capitalized on to convince the subject that human contact induces a re-experiencing of infantile catastrophe with immediate, fatal consequences. Seductive fantasy solutions to these problems are also proffered.

The second corner of the triangle is the individual's nonpsychotic thinking. No matter how insistent psychotic thinking is, provided that it does not impose suicide as a way of saving the subject's life, nonpsychotic thinking subsists and may become accessible. It can suffer a similar fate to the need for help from another person, because healthy thinking includes the need to communicate with the other, internally and externally, and so must come under attack. Psychotic edicts to withdraw, not think or talk, may be unequivocal but the psychosis cannot prevent a third party from listening, thinking or speaking. Phobically reactive to human contact, psychosis can only attempt to pervert or destroy communication by seducing or bullying the nonpsychotic mind into evading or not responding to communication from the other.

The oppressed, nonpsychotic, more healthy aspect of the mind of the subject holds tenaciously to residual sanity and the need to protect the true self, no matter how compromised or debased its efforts. To not do so amounts to self-destruction. Desperate for help, the nonpsychotic mind listens for signs of the developmental life blood of emotional intelligence from the other. Though impounded, this remaining sanity within the beleaguered personality may signal receipt of human tenderness though a glance, body movement or utterance, positive or negative. Punishment for the impiety of human contact by an enraged psychosis may follow, but acceptance of emotional intelligence gives the nonpsychotic mind an incentive to listen for something similar. The ally's principal asset in these brushes with reality is patience. Attempts to wrest more from the nonpsychotic mind than it is capable of providing will founder. If tolerant, patient, focused encounters with nonpsychotic needs are permitted, no matter how fleeting or disguised, with little or no demand made of the mind under siege, the third corner of the triangle may eventually be reached.

This corner takes the form of a connection or bridge constructed over time between the nonpsychotic minds of both protagonists. Through this link it may become possible to initiate a conversation between two sane individuals about what it feels like to be insane. Of course, it is necessary for the ally to be on good enough speaking terms with his or her insanity to avoid misunderstandings like pointless advocacy or insistent interpretation. The difference between the participants in these exchanges lies less in qualitative disparities and more in differences in intimacy with the psychotic and nonpsychotic personalities within themselves.

Crucial to the outcome of this work is a realization by the nonpsychotic personality of the subject that the ally will not engage in any altercation with the psychosis. There are many reasons for this, the most important being that psychosis and perversion are capable of inventing reality and the universe that contains reality, merely by thinking them. I think, therefore it is so. The putative ally does not have this preeminence, being restricted to the confines of ordinary reality, which is the principal asset for forging links. The capacity of the ally to survive destruction of ordinary reality in favor of psychotically invented realities is likely to instill confidence in the mind of the patient that authentic bridges, though tenuous, may survive and even grow.

When two nonpsychotic minds converse about what it is like to feel insane, it is an undertaking fraught with obstacles, two of which are quickly evident. The first is the mental and emotional pain generated by the discussion itself. The very experience of human interdependence throws into agonizing relief a gulf denoting what has been missing for so long, perhaps for as long as the individual can remember. Conversations can feel excruciating, albeit essential. The second obstacle is the deep-seated determination of the psychosis to control, berate and threaten the individual with apocalyptic visions of destruction if contact with the ally is not broken off. A mental and emotional breakdown may occur as a result of these pressures. More often than not this can be a much-needed step in recovery – *reculer pour mieux sauter*.[1]

A woman I know could not leave her abusive husband: each time she tried she fell ill and needed to be hospitalized. A routine established itself in which the husband sympathized with the hospital staff's difficulties in managing his 'crazy' wife and he promised he would take care of her.

She would be discharged with some medication and return home to be subjected to alternating humiliating punishments, threats of abandonment and seductions. Her husband knew that his wife had suffered at the hands of her psychotic mother on the isolated farm in the Midwestern United States where she was brought up. The mother had regularly threatened suicide and abandonment of her entire family – husband and six children – convinced that she was not worthy of being a wife or mother. My patient was the eldest child and became enslaved by the role of keeping her mother alive and from leaving.

Familiar with his wife's dread of losing her mother in this way, the husband exploited her fear to cruel ends, encouraging her to believe that he was the most reliable and best provider for her and to comply with him. After talking with her for a number of years including through several breakdowns, this woman came to experience that the 'nothing' to which she linked life (in her view, embrace of death) if she were not with her husband was connected to a dream-like realization that she had always believed that her mother would not survive if she (the daughter) ever separated from her. The mother had treated her daughter not as a daughter but as a substitute mother whose job it was to prevent the mother from leaving and therefore the daughter from dying. Though long dead, the mother lived on in her in the guise of the husband, with whom she relived a version of her incarcerated childhood: neither he nor she could survive separation from each other, she believed. She had sacrificed her life to her mother and now to her husband. Through a series of small steps deriving from insights into these dilemmas, like spending weekends away, making a friend or two and above all being emotionally honest with herself about her situation, she came to see that the 'nothing' she feared if she were to leave her husband was, in reality, 'something' when contrasted with the so-called something promised by him, which amounted, in reality, to nothing more than his living parasitically off her. To address her delusional dependence on this mother-figure, she needed to acquire her own version of what I have elsewhere termed euphemistically a 'Fuck It' attitude.

In a previous publication (Williams, 2010) I describe a 'fifth principle' required for a radical shift in forms of relating needed by individuals like the woman above, if fundamental and lasting change is to occur. Although colloquially termed *'Fuck It'*, this principle is not a simple rejection of past experiences but a dismantling of the very terms upon which such ways of relating have been constructed and continue their destructiveness into the present. The superficial use of the phrase *'Fuck It'* refers to an attack on the power of another and an attempt to reverse who is powerful and who is helpless. This master–slave interaction fails to generate change, simply alternating or reversing dominance and submissiveness. A radical *'Fuck It'* rejection of underlying terms of relating that use power, manipulation, terror and control of another, culminating in insanity, is the sense in which the term is being used here. This is both difficult and far-reaching because a new set of terms is needed to be created to replace those based on the abuse of power and which can augur freedom of the subject to do what they want, which is not harmful to anyone, including themselves. This cannot be achieved alone. It is nothing short of a revolution in the life of the hitherto debased, self-incarcerated individual. It may require a continuous finding and re-finding of the new premises for relating as different destructive circumstances present themselves and before they settle into something approaching an integral attitude.

Even then, we can be vulnerable to oppressive situations and may revert to old ways of responding. What makes it possible to deal with events differently is an anchoring of ourselves in new terms of relating forged to maintain dignity through honesty and nonengagement with abusive forms of power.

Another way of putting this is to imagine the authority of tenderness as applied to oneself and others. This is not be confused with sentimentality or niceness. The authority of tenderness generates change from nonviolent confrontation with hatred, rage and suffering within oneself and others which, if sufficiently thorough, yields heartfelt repudiation of their malignant origins. By embracing the worst in us and others we embrace the best in us, because this is the foundation of humanity born of raw feelings of need, love and hatred. In the psychotic domain of slaughter, perdition and seduction human forms of relating are unavailable. To obtain them it is necessary for me to kill my psychotic murderers not with cruelty or using their methods but with the authority of tenderness. This is a weapon about which they know nothing and even less how to withstand, because there is nothing to withstand. The authority of tenderness, which is active, not passive, deprives psychotic figures of the oxygen they need for their flames of destruction. They cannot engage with the lack of panic at the heart of the authority of tenderness and they fall short of their target when desecration is received, even invited, into a living room they would not countenance entering. Confronting the influence of murderers may proceed steadfastly, with the assistance of the patient, in a triangle, now hopefully a relationship, until, sapped of their absolutism, the psychotic attacks struggle increasingly to properly ignite. The authority of unflinching tenderness that is aggressive but not destructive

76

or submissive derives from its alignment with the patient's unique truth – more accurately, two unique truths in collaboration and occasionally in alignment. Psychosis is, if nothing else, tenacious. The therapeutic task is the modification of seduction, excoriation and murderousness into abeyance, rage, grief and connection. The depleted individual unjustly fashioned into a murderer, under murderous circumstances, may become freer to begin to live a life, not merely survive an existence. They are *no longer isolated or alone*. Their psychic investments, so to speak, can begin to shift, little by little, away from the bank of psychosis to a more ordinary bank run by people.

Without help to find their own personal rendering of this *'Fuck It'* principle, their humanity is unlikely to be resuscitated.

Note

1 To draw back in order to make a better leap forward.

10

FUCK IT ALL

There is a category of person for whom the most apt and respectful epithet is killed. Circumstances during development have been such that relational and emotional qualities were wiped out or failed to establish themselves. Individuals diagnosed with certain variants of 'schizophrenia' may fall into this category, but it is not confined to the overtly, psychiatrically ill. Killed people may occupy jobs – even important jobs; they may be wives or husbands, mothers or fathers. What they share in common is the dilemma of the dead: an experience of inner annihilation. It is a state of nonexistence against which they believe themselves to be powerless, no matter how hard they oppose it, as though they have lost or had stolen from them or never had something integral – a capacity to experience themselves as persons. Differentiation from or disagreement with others or the world, let alone the capacity to rebel, except perhaps against themselves, is missing. Their demeanor may be cooperative and seemingly rational, if lifeless. Cognition may have been dragooned into managing life's difficulties. Some appear to think, perform tasks and exhibit reasonable levels of competence deriving from adaptation and

DOI: 10.4324/9781003176862-10

rationalization, but intelligent decisions are unmakeable. When faced with obstacles, they employ received opinion and approximation through memory. This is not false: it is the sole resource they have available.

A killed person may seem capable in a crisis, having managed crises of unmanageable proportions. They can appear to be normal whilst beset by profound, unrelenting dread regarding the toxicity of the world and, in particular, themselves. They feel appallingly insubstantial and meaningless yet radioactive in their capacity to contaminate others. They flee from barrenness by becoming workaholics or chronic helpers or may abuse substances or develop debilitating illnesses. Overt behavior, to which they cleave ritualistically, is carefully circumscribed to keep them above the abyss of defeat and annihilation. Killed individuals know that something went impossibly wrong, yet at the same time they do not know what it was. Generalizing about the nature of their defeat is not possible or desirable. At best one might say it is something akin to excruciating poisonousness generated by not being fully, rightfully dead. Mental illness, an agony in itself, is more tolerable than annihilation, which is why being killed can lie behind a variety of different psychiatric disorders and be so difficult to identify.

It is likely that there is no single set of circumstances or experiences that can accounts for being killed. Their experience may arise in different developmental contexts and yield symptoms and disorders of different kinds. One unifying factor is a sense of ongoing helplessness in the face of feelings of permanent annihilation. Traumatizing thoughts of being killed or assailed may recur, mechanical thinking and behavior may prevail, passivity may be prominent or, physically, they may experience symptoms like tics, heart murmur, irritable bowel syndrome, eczema or other physical pains. Paranoid rituals, slave-like compliance and disengagement may occur. These individuals are in a parlous position compared to those able to exhibit some assertiveness, aggression, disagreement or rebellion whilst suffering a psychiatric or severe psychological condition. The latter are attached to life in a way the former are not. The relationship of the killed to therapeutic help is equally parlous. A journey back or forward to becoming human, something the true self sanctions and needs, is fraught with the catastrophe of disaffiliation. Loss of the soul, experiences of perdition, compulsive self-sacrifice and a yearning for death militate strongly against change. In addition, there is the poorly investigated dilemma of the pain of change for individuals who have been deformed by too much injurious change.

For a viable individual – a person – the pain of facing reality is assuaged by inner and outer affiliations that facilitate and support the undertaking. When a killed person faces the pain of change, instead of using the mind as an organ to deliver sensorial numbness, the scale of lamentation is such that self-immolation and disintegration are risks. Death-in-life is viewed as more tenable than life or affiliation. The therapeutic help the killed require, aside from infinite patience, lies in addressing an exaltation of death and their belief in an infinity capacity to inflict death on others. Although associated with notions like omnipotence and omniscience, these ideas fail to address the visceral experience of being killed. The body as well as the mind no longer functions as it should, if it ever did, a capacity to function being a faint memory or fantasy masquerading as memory.

Being killed is a shame-filled matter of disastrous proportions. The killed feel they have been killed and kill as an inborn endowment. They do not want it, despise themselves for it and cannot explain why they were killed or kill. That this is distorted thinking is unquestionable, but this is not at all the experience of the killed. What shocks them in life, at least until their situation is accepted, is that their inhumanity is most visible when least expected, in circumstances where calm or a risk of satisfaction presents itself. A conversation or, worse, an act of kindness is followed by an electrical storm of reflexive hatred (experienced one or both ways). A familiar but vicious conviction of abhorrence gives way to impossible dismay and the need to physically and mentally disappear. The iniquity of the situation cannot be explained by misguided aggression, although this is involved. The experience of the killed is a feeling of innate, pervasive deadliness, a constitutional disfigurement of cells that desecrates them and everything else, propelling them towards suicide. Encouragement to repudiate or question their lethality hastens their demise. Until acceptance by an independent silent witness occurs of the truth that any utterance, touch, glance, breath or feeling by the killed kills, startling the perpetrator and the world each time, the disease will hold fast. It is art, in the form of an unhurried, unknown picture painted of the conditions for carnage, that may eventually offer the killed a different experience of an ordinary, not perverse, split second of illumination.

In order for the killed to be killed and killer (the latter in toxic, radioactive form rather than intentional violence), certain experiences have occurred. These can only be approximated using broad brush strokes, the nature of the subject's lethality requiring a thoroughgoing analysis according to the circumstances of the killings, a project that must always be thought of as impossible in order to have any likelihood of fruition. In short, two experiences bring about killing and being killed. One is dependence, a universal, helpless state which, if treated as a toxic demand, merits scorn and destruction. The subject's need to stay alive is killed. Untenable, the situation provokes the need for dependence to assert itself, which is killed. The subject is responsible for a malignant trait – the disgrace of dependence – and is killed, and if objection to the indictment arises, this is killed. The subject is responsible for two malignant traits – expression of need and expression of objection – two elemental components of being alive killed for their lethality. Differences between subject and object are totally confused save for virtue, which pertains to the object. Stretched on a rack, the subject is unable to move in any direction.

One option remains and that is to disappear. Disappearance takes the form of radical withdrawal by the authentic self into deepest concealment, shrouded by an effigy of a mortal. From this time on, appearance signals death on the two prevailing counts: toxic, radioactive killing of others through need and protest that the disaster is an error. To be saved from killing and being killed, the subject remains immobile on the rack, because any movement increases torture. There is no way out. More accurately, there was, is and never will be a way out for the killed.

There may come to pass in the silence the possibility of the smallest of observations from an unknown perspective that may, with help, gain credence. Acceptance, in full, of having been killed is the precondition for the observation, a point of view that is inconceivable and necessary. Death was real, as is the wasteland, as is the lingering effigy. Awareness of these realities calls for assistance of single-hearted character from the silent witness in order to admit the inadmissible reality of bereavement of the self, with no petition for clemency or compensation. Admission of the cult of killing and being killed, its justification the satiating thrills of butchery, and a lust for limitless dominion allow for a different quality of cessation of movement on the rack and therefore of killing and being killed. Defenseless on the rack, a survey of a scene of universal carnage over which we had and have no influence or control may begin.

The 'Fuck It' principle quoted earlier sought the dismantling and replacement of the very terms of destructive ways of relating as they persisted from the past into the present. For the killed individual this may be of help but it is ultimately not enough. The condition for life was the experience of death, a culture of killing producing a carrier of radioactive death deserving only of extermination. Whichever direction the subject faces, death appears, beginning within himself. Acceptance, not of deadly actions but of a universe of death, is not possible yet is necessary. The single-hearted collaborative aid alluded to earlier must endorse an eternity of silence at the scale of this privation. This delicate variant of a reprieve may engender faint notes of discrimination needed for acceptance of a universe of death. Unthinkable though this seems, notes of discrimination not only expedite heartbreak at this universe but constitute elements of a radical awareness that there is only one sane perspective available in the face of such annihilation, and that is destruction of the universe. Such notes of discrimination are responsible for the universe of death no longer being the entire universe, its dominion notwithstanding. It becomes clear over time that the rack has not been constructed to torture attentive silence or acceptance. Discrimination allows for, from the other side of this black hole of isolation, consideration of an eventual dream of what death might not be, with the potential for refinement of judgement this brings. In grief, hatred and acceptance, the subject may discern, then grasp, a single, previously unrecognized remaining lifeline in his possession – destruction of the universe of death.

This is far from a clear or linear process. Destruction of the universe requires intolerance of everyone and everything. A frontier is established through which life, not death, may pass. It requires a 'Fuck It All' principle less related to delinquency and more to an ethical, moral frame of reference for aggressive, humane commitment to contesting and overturning toxicity. It culminates, with enough deliberation and support, in the authority of tenderness in a distilled form. The discriminatory power of the authority of tenderness, forged from a reflective preparedness for an exacting engagement with death and destruction, embraces the worst in us, and therefore is the best in us. From it emerges acceptance of life forms from the slightest to the most heartfelt.

If this is not a cause for celebration, what is?

REFERENCES

Borges, J. L. (1970) *The Aleph and Other Stories*. New York: E.P. Dutton.

Johnson, T. H. (1961) *The Complete Poems of Emily Dickinson*. New York: Back Bay Books.

Lanzmann, C. (1985) *Shoah*. New Yorker Films.

Levi, P. (2003*) If This Is a Man and The Truce*. London: Abacus.

Marquis de Sade. (2016) *The One Hundred and Twenty Days of Sodom*. London: Penguin Classics.

Montaigne, M. (1949) *Essays*. Translated and Edited by W. C. Hazlitt. New York: Modern Library.

O'Connor, F. (1969) *Mystery and Manners: Occasional Prose*. Selected and edited by Sally and Robert Fitzgerald. London: Macmillan.

Williams, P. (2010) *The Fifth Principle*. London: Karnac Books.

Williams, P. (2014) Orientations of psychotic activity in defensive pathological organizations. *The International Journal of Psychoanalysis*, *95*(3), 423–444.

Winnicott, D. W. W. (1963) Communicating and not communicating leading to a study of certain opposites. In M. Masud Khan (Ed.), *The Maturational Processes and the Facilitating Environment: Studies in the Theory of Emotional Development*, pp. 179–192. London: The International Psycho-Analytic Library.

INDEX

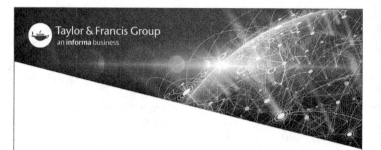

Printed in the United States
by Baker & Taylor Publisher Services